CONTENTS

A
comprehensive
education
1965-1975

A comprehensive education 1965-1975

Roger Mills

Centerprise Trust Ltd.

Copyright 1978 Roger Mills
Published by Centerprise Trust Ltd,
136 Kingsland High Street, London E8.
Typeset by Bread 'n Roses.
Printed by Expression Printers Ltd, London.
Centerprise Trust Ltd is grateful for financial assistance from
Hackney Borough Council,
the Greater London Arts Association, and the
Inner London Education Authority.
ISBN 0 903738 37 6

Centerprise is a member of the
Federation of Worker Writers and
Community Publishers.

Introduction 1965

The public schools were so good, one teacher told us, that boys came from all over the world just to be a pupil at even the most obscure of them. Well, it seemed to me that our school must be on some sort of par with them, because we had boys from all over the world at our school too. We had boys from the West Indies, Pakistan, Malta, Italy, Greece, Cyprus, Africa and Turkey, and that's not forgetting the boys from the nearer places — Scotland, Ireland and Wales. Boys, hundreds of them from all over the globe, all sent to Britain and all converging in that one building at the top of Effingham Road in Hackney.

1965 to 1975? You weren't at school that long were you? No! Of course not. I left in 1971. My seemingly peculiar dating comes about because in 1975 I found myself out of work and for the first time reflecting on my life up until then. I felt I had left a person behind who I would never be again, someone who had experienced things I could now begin to interpret and try to make sense of. I felt a time had come when rather than continually absorbing I could give something back, hence this autobiography. I included a few incidents which, although I had left school, could certainly be called educational.

I really don't know whether this book would have been written at all if Centerprise didn't exist. As most people reading this will already know Centerprise is a community bookshop, coffee bar and publishing project in Hackney. It was there I discovered 'local' authors. To discover that working class people were writing and being taken seriously was a revelation to me. I'd thought I must be the only one. I had been writing short pieces before I knew about Centerprise. Without the opportunity offered there though, I think it's likely I would not still be writing. I would especially like to thank Ken Worpole at Centerprise. Funnily enough he was the first person I had ever showed any of my work to. I never showed it to parents or friends. I was too shy. It was Ken who introduced me to the Stepney Basement writers who I have been involved with ever since. Ken couldn't see any reason why I shouldn't write an autobiography and when I stopped finding reasons why I shouldn't I went straight ahead, writing on note pads and bits of paper, on the tube, in buses and at home. Thanks also to Wilma Pennycook who worked so hard on the typing of my handwritten manuscript.

I had gone to Effingham Road School an eleven year old, I came out a young man just over five years later; we all had. This autobiography was written with that in mind. Any one of the thousand boys there could have written this story, only maybe they would have different interpretations and put more emphasis on things I may have missed out altogether. Names have been changed to protect the innocent and guilty alike.

I started in the summer of 1965. I was frightened and unprepared. I felt that school was something preventing me from joining the new 'Swinging London' outside. It was the era of the Beatles, the new Labour government, Mary Quant and the mini skirt. The number one record was 'Satisfaction'.

> 'I can't get no satisfaction,
> And I try, and I try,
> And I try, and I try.'

Roger Mills

First day

I was waiting in the school's reception area. Teachers and boys alike passed and looked down their noses at me inquisitively. I had only been here once before, with my parents while awaiting my interview. It had gone pretty smoothly. I had read from a book, tried my best to get a few sums right and answered questions on general knowledge.

I could never see the point of the interview with its questions and everything, as the purpose of the school was to teach you all the answers you didn't know anyway.

A tearless farewell from primary school and a long hot six weeks holiday culminating in a sleepless last night had resulted in my sitting outside the administrative offices of Effingham Road Comprehensive School. Actually, due to a previously booked holiday, I missed the first week at Effingham Road and for ever after wondered if I had missed some vital explanation during that week, some single phrase or few words which would have made everything add up, made everything clear and given some meaning and reason for the next five years I would spend here.

All I had actually missed was a guided tour on the first day. The first year boys, without the hindrance of the other years, who started the next day, were shown the wonders of the premises. The school was just five years old. It was the Phoenix out of the flames of a couple of old mixed schools which lost the girls on the way.

On their tour the boys were shown the three huge buildings which made up the school. The main block, the largest, contained all the classrooms, the chemistry laboratories, large art rooms, lecture theatre, staff rooms and toilets on all three floors. That was a bit different from my primary school where we had to pee in the outside toilet while the rain came in through the roof. Everything here was clean and modern.

The next largest block contained the hall. It was enormous with a real stage, curtains and lighting, and a high, high roof. The hall was sandwiched between two gymnasiums, north and south respectively. The gyms were fully equipped with climbing bars, punchbags, lifting weights, jumping horses and ropes to the ceiling. Opposite, past the fenced-in playground and beside the bikesheds, was the smallest of the three blocks, the 'Technical Block' as it was called. It housed classes for plumbing, carpentry, brick-laying and metal work.

Besides all this it was rumoured that there was even a tuck shop.

But I had missed out on that tour and it was three years before I knew my way about the school. Now I was alone with my brand new briefcase, empty save for a fountain pen. There was no group of boys to hide behind and no friends to share my worries with. I was awaiting the man whom a kind voiced secretary told me would take me to join my class. My heart pumped. The man was the Deputy Headmaster, an old man who spoke to me only briefly, very formally, in a squeaky voice.

He led me up to the first floor, head down as if deep in thought, not looking to check if I was still here behind him. In the long corridor, through the small glass panels by the classroom doors, I could see teachers taking registers. All the boys were clothed in the school uniform of black trousers and blazers, white shirts and school ties.

The six classes in the first year were given the initials of the tutor master, the one who marked the register morning and afternoon. I was in 1M: Miss Munroe.

The Deputy Headmaster introduced me, exchanged a few brief words with her and left. Miss Munroe was a pleasant woman of about twenty-five. She had long black hair and wore a short dress. She had large features and was not particularly pretty in the conventional way. Being an all boys school however, she was soon to become our sex symbol. At lunchtimes and at lesson changes groups of boys would gather at the bottom of the stairs to look up her skirt.

Miss Munroe welcomed me with a polite smile and a blank timetable. 'Look at four eyes!' someone called. She silenced whoever it was and found me a seat. The boys around me tried to convince me that I was in Livingstone House. I knew I was in Scott House, though, because my tie was blue. The other boys in the room sported red, blue, green or yellow ties denoting which house they belonged to. Before now I had thought that like in 'Goodbye Mr. Chips' we would only see the boys from the other houses for Sportsday or punchups; that didn't seem to be the case however.

Looking around the class I saw that nearly all the boys were as well turned out as I was. A few of the boys' blazers were obviously hand-me-downs years old. Doubtless if I had had an elder brother my uniform would not have been as brand new as it was.

On being accepted to the school my family had received a list of clothes required and a choice of just two places to get them. Besides the basic uniform I was told I must have a sports vest, shorts and plimsolls, a cap that nobody ever wore, a regulation pullover and an apron for technical work.

The very uniforms themselves gave the boys a frightening anonymity. No more short trousers and woolies that you always got milk on. We all looked like young bankers. There was just one boy wearing short trousers, a very small boy who made up in cunning what he lacked in physique. He had already made friends with Sammy Johnson, a ginger haired boy and at eleven one of the school's tallest inhabitants, pupil or teacher. At five feet eleven he was the only first year not to get picked on in the playground.

The boy next to me explained the tutor groups. Shortly we would be going to assembly and then straight on to our various lessons. Every lesson a change of room, a change of teacher, not at all like primary school. Besides now and early afternoon we would not see Miss Munroe again except for French. I could tell she was a French teacher because of the corny posters of Paris on the back wall and the hand written sign 'Bibliotheque' above a row of two books on a shelf.

The timetable that Miss Munroe had given me was a blank white card divided into five sections downward marked: Monday, Tuesday, Wednesday, Thursday and Friday. More lines, horizontal, split the card into seven sections, period one down to period seven. Seven periods of lessons, five days a week. Four periods in the morning split by break (they didn't call it playtime here) and three in the afternoon after two sittings of lunch. Hometime was three-forty; well that couldn't be bad anyway.

The boy beside me lent me his timetable, already creased and supple after just one week. Under my name I religiously copied out the name of each lesson in its correct space. While busily writing I saw a definite pattern emerging. An order of importance. We had five periods a week of both Mathematics and English (five periods = three hours and twenty minutes) while of subjects such as music we received just one.

Suddenly, and to nobody's surprise but mine, a box on the wall began to talk. It had a plummy middle aged voice which told teachers to prepare the classes and bring them down to assembly. The box on the wall, one of which lived in every room also let out three bleeps or pips every time we had to change lessons. Sometimes if we were lucky we could hear the people inside it discussing the school when they forgot to switch off. We even got Radio Caroline through it once.

As we banged our desks and scraped our chairs along the floor to line up by the door in twos, I noticed with instant

nausea what the first lesson of my whole secondary school career was to be, according to the timetable:
Maths.
There in plain black and white.
Maths.
No argument.
Maths.
No mistake.

Assembly? I didn't notice that for worry. In no time at all I found myself in an orderly if nervous queue outside room 101 right on the top floor. I was hot and then cold. Ever since I could remember I had had a sort of mental block where Arithmetic was concerned. I never got past the two times table. In primary school the other children would confidently rattle all the tables off in unison while I mimed them. I was terrified that any moment I would be stood up on a chair and commanded to perform them solo.

Now again I pictured in my mind humiliation being doled out mercilessly by some smooth, acid-witted, shark-faced teacher while the rest of the boys rolled around in hysterics at this total idiot a week late and already five years behind.

The teacher turned out to be short and fat and apart from providing me with a text and exercise book made no acknowledgement of my previous absence. To my horror I was placed just a row from the front, too close for comfort. I don't know if the division sums he gave me were easy or hard, my mind was a thick fog and I could not even begin to work them out. It was all just numbers, it made no sense.

A glance at the boy's book beside me made him cup his hand over the page. I felt like shouting for help. To my great relief the small boy told the teacher he didn't know how to do the work, something I was afraid to do. After tutting and making a few chalk marks on the board however the short fat teacher still made me none the wiser. I merely wrote the questions out as neatly as possible in the hope of leniency. I did the elementary parts I knew how to do and even made a wild guess at some of the answers. None was correct.

Whatever my punishment was to be I was consoled in the thought that it would be postponed for a few days until the books were marked. It was not to be. At about ten minutes from the end of the forty minute period everybody began to line up either side of the teacher's desk to have their books marked. I was hot again now and actually felt a little sick. I stood last in the line hoping those funny pips would save me. They didn't, and being the last made it all the worse. The teacher was jibing and complaining about the boys' work and the state of their books and when I put my one down he exploded. There was not one complete sum and after all my neat setting out I had smudged the lot with my sleeve.

'What do you call this?' he asked.

'I'm not very well, sir,' I lied.

'I'm not very well either,' he lied back, 'But I do what's expected of me. If you couldn't do the work why the devil didn't you tell me?'

I felt my face go bright red and heard some sniggering from behind me.

'If you come here next time and sit there doing nothing then I'll do something about you. As it's your first time here however I'll let it pass. You make sure you do your homework though, and that goes for all of you,' he said, thankfully taking the attention from me at the end.

'It's everything on page twelve of your text book.'

Homework? I had never had any of that before at my primary school. I figured at least I could get my father to help me on that one though, so I was not worried. I crammed my books into my briefcase and was pleased to get out of that room.

Come breaktime the corridor was a racetrack of large and small boys. They were all making a dash for the playground as if their lives depended on the seconds they might miss in the yard.

I saw Danny in the chewing gum spattered yard. Danny was a boy who lived just over the road to me who I walked to school with. We had been friends for a long time and it was partially due to him that I got my parents to put down Effingham Road as first choice of school. But he was with his second year friends now, he had served his apprenticeship in the first. I did not speak to him. I was just a weedy first year.

I put my bag down on the ground between my legs, my hands in my pockets and leaned up against the high wire which partitioned off the main playground area. Then BOING, I went hurtling forward like a sling shot and landed on the floor. Some big boys on the other side of the fence walked off laughing. I did not fall into the arms of Jamie and Paul but it was they who picked me up.

Jamie was the boy whom I had sat beside in tutor group and Paul was his friend who sat at the back.

'Now that was yer first mistake,' said Jamie, 'Never ever lean up against the wire.'

'Why did they do that?' I said. The question made no

sense to Jamie and Paul but eventually Paul said 'Because you were there, that's all.'

'You better watch out for your bag an' all mate,' said Jamie. Watch out they don't nick it an' bung it down the toilet, or they might hide it.'

'Worse still' said Paul, 'They just stamp on it from behind when you're carrying it so that it's torn out of you hand. It really hurts your fingers.'

'I'll get them if they do,' I said with mock bravery.

'Nah' said Jamie 'it's not worth it if they are bigger than you. There's a lot of really nasty geezers about this place.'

It seemed you only had to be here a week to be a veteran. They told me all about the bullies and how you must never 'tell' to a teacher. It was an unwritten rule. They told me all about Mr. Price too and how Jamie had already been caned by him.

Jamie was a wiry, dark curly-headed boy, very lively and always darting about ferret-like. He never seemed to take much care of his bag.

'That's the secret,' he told me. 'If you protect it like a bloody baby of course everyone will try to nick it. There's this one kid, Keyhole Kate we call 'im 'cos of 'is conk, puts his chairleg through the 'andle so's it's nailed to the floor. You get boys crawling under desks and tables like commandos trying to get it off him. If, though, you slouch about with your bag open and all filthy, fling it in a corner and leave it unprotected while you go for a Jimmy Riddle then absolutely nobody bothers to touch it.'

Paul was quite different — taller than us with tidy short hair, he gave the appearance of a trainee head-boy, blazer and bag the smartest, and face free of spots. He was no twit though, otherwise he would never have got on with Jamie.

Both Paul and Jamie were Livingstone Boys, so I would be alone again in the Scott dining room. I had always shied away from dinners at primary school because after sliding them up and down the long shiny topped tables you ended up with somebody else's half finished meal. But here things were strictly organized and on my first day I had meat, peas and a hard lump of mashed potato.

It seemed well worth the shilling though. Afters, I was told, was always something with custard. Today was no exception. I walked back from the serving hatch very carefully, watching the floating apple crumble slop from side to side in the deep dish. I placed it on the table and leaned forward to sit on my chair. My tie turned yellow as it dangled in the custard and then stuck to my shirt as I sat down. I wiped it off with the new handkerchief my mother had put in my pocket and after the laughter had died down I tasted it. It wasn't bad.

Lunch was finished off with a quarter-pint bottle of milk. If you sat on the end tables though you didn't always get one because the milk monitors had stolen it.

The thing that struck me most on that first day was the newness of everything. Everything steel and glass, everything white and clean. It had none of the cosiness of my primary classroom with its rabbits at the back and painted pictures on the wall. Lesson changes here were hustle and bustle, aggressive shoulders pushing in the corridors and bodies jostling on the stairs.

The afternoon passed uneventfully with lessons like History and Geography, things I could handle. The teachers seemed very reasonable and much more helpful than the Maths teacher had been.

It was a very long day, the way it always is when you are in totally new surroundings and your mind does not get a chance to slip into routine. I arrived home, legs aching — it was over a mile's walk. My arms ached too, my bag full of fat hardback books with torn pages. A new worry was stirring in my mind, all that homework. Homework kept you from playing in the streets or watching television.

But I did watch television that evening of the first day. On a variety show a comedian told the joke about the little boy after his first day at primary school. His mother said 'Now we're not going to have all that crying and screaming when you go tomorrow are we?' and he said, 'You don't mean I have to go again, do you?'

The long arm law

Bullying & discipline

The Long Arm Law stated that anybody big enough to bully you did bully you and therefore had the right to bully you. If teachers got you to do what they commanded then they had the right; if they couldn't then they didn't. Probably the most successful enforcer of the Long Arm Law was Mr. Price. Mr. Price was a tall curly-haired man of about fifty. According to others he was a reasonable, good natured man while teaching his sixth form English students. He hated first years.

There was nowhere outside Mr. Price's jurisdiction. He would tell boys off on the stairs for whistling, in the dinner room for talking and in the playground for playing. To him childhood was something to be cured of.

The first time I encountered him was about a month into that first term. We were all cavorting and yelling in the hall's entrance waiting for the Drama teacher to arrive. Suddenly Mr. Price, like Moses discovering the party going on at the bottom of the mountain, loomed at the doorway hands at angry sides.

'Get in order at once!' he bellowed, 'You awful children.'

The result was as quick as it was amazing. Like a tangled ball of string pulled taut into perfect unknotted order all the boys jumped into correct position. Position of class, height, age, size of shoes, just about everything to appease the wrath of this unknown avenger.

Everyone that is except for me. It was all so astounding that I stood where I was rooted to the floor, perfectly still amidst the panic with a smile on my face.

Soon I was balancing on my toes, my top button popping and my face tomato red. Mr. Price, on seeing this insolent wretch with a smirk on his face, had grabbed me by the knot of the tie and hauled me up.

'Do you think it's funny?' he shouted at point blank range. Now he may have been a hard man or even a violent man but at least he had given me a choice. I could either lie and be set free with nothing but a scolding or I could tell the truth, 'Yes, I thought it was bloody hilarious', and receive a caning at the very least.

'No sir,' I told him.

In my early years at Effingham Road School discipline was maintained with a stick. It appeared out of desks, out of cupboards, behind blackboards and in Mr. Joyce's case, from up his sleeve. He was my housemaster. He would keep it up there while patrolling the corridors and when required, when he found some rowdy boys, he would let it drop and catch it by the end ready for action.

Some teachers would have a cane sent for. It would be brought ceremoniously back from the headmaster's office by an unwilling dupe while in the classroom tension mounted up like in an Alfred Hitchcock film.

In extreme cases the headmaster himself would be sent for, arriving like the cavalry to rescue some poor student teacher. The headmaster was a plump, bald, sixty-year-old man. He almost always wore his black cloak, a black suit and a sardonic expression. He was scrupulously fair when it came to punishment. He was convinced of the righteousness of the stick and had a scale of punishments. One on the hand for what he called 'natural schoolboy mischieveousness' and anything up to three whacks on the backside for something he considered bad.

The headmaster's presence alone was enough to guarantee servile silence. Nobody dared breathe loudly for fear of being cast as conspirator in whatever had been going on. His slow movements and dark brown deliberate speech made us shake at the knees, quake at the boots and more.

It was a knack not peculiar to the headmaster though; some teachers had it, some had not. Some teachers could and would stand at the head of the class and threaten, scream and cajole but still have a riot on their hands. No matter what they tried, no order came from chaos. There were certain teachers though, like Mr. Price, who only had to be in the room to maintain a churchyard silence. His strong body and hawk eye were the calm before the storm, a deceptive stillness that a shrug or sneer could transform into a thrashing, gesticulating, shouting torrent of teacher.

Mr. Price walking in the corridor meant everybody else walking in the corridor, not jumping, running and fighting as usual. Boys lolling outside their classes were immediately crisp neat rows on just hearing his footsteps. The library, where boys pored over 'Sgt Fury', was suddenly an intellectual temple with boys clutching Shakespeare and Shaw just at the mention of his name.

However, whereas Mr. Price's anger could be seen coming from his facial contortions, other teachers were not so predictable.

Mr. Sharpe was a stickler for discipline; he was also a bit of a legend. It was rumoured that he was an ex-public school teacher who was dismissed for his excessive punishment.

His sadism it was said, stemmed from the war years when his family were completely wiped out by enemy bombs. It was also rumoured that he was expressly banned from using the cane.

To us he was an unknown quantity; apart from his habit of clutching his jaw and stretching it down as if it were elastic, we didn't know him. We were only awaiting his arrival now because our usual Maths teacher was away. When he arrived he stood before us in Sgt. Major stance with hands behind his back.

'I don't want to hear one word spoken as we go in the room,' he said quietly, and he led us in. Of course somebody spoke: Sammy Johnson, the ginger giant.

Mr. Sharpe was cool and collected. He ordered Sammy to stand at the head of the class while the rest of us found our seats. He kept an eye on us all. When all was silent Mr. Sharpe stood before Sammy and merely said, 'Good, I like big boys.'

Whaccck!

What had happened? With frightening speed and force Mr. Sharpe had brought a hand round from behind his back and slapped Sammy's incredulous face. He was sent sprawling helplessly into a row of desks. They crashed and shifted as with ruby red face he tried to find his feet. Too frightened to look back at his aggressor he retreated clumsily to his desk. Sammy looked like at any moment he might pass out. He didn't, but sat slouched throughout the whole lesson trembling like a thrashed dog.

His authority well and truly asserted, Mr. Sharpe returned to his seat, happy in the knowledge not one boy would dare to as much as cough in the ensuing forty minutes.

After the lesson a few of us encouraged Sammy to go and tell the headmaster. We knew our rights, or so we thought. You cannot slap a pupil around the face. Sammy did go, later in the afternoon when fear had turned to indignity. He didn't get much satisfaction though. 'Forgive him this time,' was the theme of the headmaster's talk.

It was not just the teachers who enforced the Long Arm Law. Of course, there were always the bullies, mostly second, third and fourth years. The bullies would always pick on you if you got in their way, bumped into them or even looked at them. All over the place it seemed big oafs were treading on your feet, twisting your arm and asking 'Do you want your 'ead punched in?' There was no answer to that really.

Home work

I was crying but not bawling. Tears of frustration were

18

running down my face.

'It's no good, I can't do it,' I mumbled and threw my books across the room. I was doing my homework in the kitchen.

'What's the matter now?' asked my mother finishing the washing up.

'It's that homework again isn't it. You'll have to control that temper of yours or you'll never get anywhere. I'll go and get your dad to help you.'

'What's the point,' I said, 'it doesn't make any sense, and besides they didn't have fractions when dad was at school.'

That first year we got more homework than in any other year. In most subjects I could get away with rehashing what the teacher had told us during the lesson. I even did it in the playground just before the lesson started. But Maths though, Maths was something else.

My father must have been the most patient man in the world. My mother went upstairs to get him where he was watching television and very soon he was leafing through my Arithmetic books and learning Pythagorus right from scratch just to help me. We worked all night, pausing for just half an hour so I could watch the Tony Hancock Show. I always liked Tony Hancock.

My mother came down to make the late night drink and we were only just finishing.

'What are you like in your other subjects?' my father asked tentatively.

'Alright,' I said and left it at that.

'Science and History,' he persisted, 'things like that, how do you do in those?'

'About average I s'pose' I told him. 'In History though, all we've been doing is Ancient Egyptians. I asked the teacher when we were going to do World War Two an' things like that and he said in the Sixth Form. I mean it's stupid, I'll be left by then.'

'You don't know,' said my mother. 'You don't know how you'll feel by then.'

'It's the teachers I think,' said my father.

'Uh?'

'The teachers. There's no other reason that Roger can't do the work. He's not thick, it must be the teachers, they're too young now. They don't command the discipline and respect.'

'Oh I don't know, Fred,' said my mother looking sideways at him. 'That Mr. Joyce we met at the meeting — he seems a firm man, I think he's got money you know.'

'Yea, I bet he has,' I said, 'he's got loads of cameras and does fencing. He's a bit posh, though.'

'Never mind that,' my father said, 'if he considers it worth his time trying to ram a bit of culture into you lot then you should be grateful. They're not silly these rich people y'know, they go to special schools.'

'Those prefects are nice smart boys,' said my mother thinking of the Sixth Form, 'perhaps you'll be one one day.'

'No fear,' I said, 'I wouldn't be one of them.'

'Just listen to the boy, he doesn't like anybody,' my father said. 'What's wrong with the damned prefects?'

'Oh, they're not so bad, I s'pose,' I conceded. 'They get pretty bossy but at least they don't bully you like some of the others.'

'What do you mean?' said my father. 'You're not being bullied are you?'

'No, well no more than anyone else ......'

'No more than anyone else! Listen, if anyone bullies you, I want to hear that you've given as good as you've got. They used to say when I was a kid 'It's not the size of the dog in the fight, it's the size of the fight in the dog.'

'It's probably just rowdiness,' piped up my mother. 'It being an all boys ......'

'No, no it's better like that,' interrupted father. 'In a mixed school everybody is trying to show off in front of the girls. A boy can't concentrate with girls in the room.'

'I don't know Fred, at least they keep a check on their bad language.'

All the boys at school swore and I began to as well. I had to constantly check myself at home to make sure I did not swear in front of my parents. There was nothing but dirty jokes either, not all of which I understood. When everybody else laughed, I laughed too.

'I remember when I was a lad,' began my father, 'it was my first day at school, you had to be tough in those days....'

'Anyway, I think you've done enough tonight Roger,' said my mother, 'time for bed.'

Danny never seemed to have any trouble with his homework. He was out every evening playing football with Christaki over the common. Christaki was a Cypriot boy the same age as Danny with a little brother, Dimmi, constantly in tow. Christaki had applied for Effingham Road School and had got as far as an interview. He was rejected and went to Daniel Defoe, a school with a terrible reputation. He would leave his house in the morning and walk around the streets; he hardly ever went to school.

I found out later the reason why Danny never had any trouble with his homework — he never did any. He was always getting wacked for it. I always thought it did not matter to him though, he had his running and football. He was such a good runner that the head of the P.E. Department would often rescue him from some boring English lesson so that he could do extra training.

Every year we had Inter-house Sports events at Victoria Park. For the Housemasters, and Danny, it was a day of glory and honour. For most of the boys who were herded there it was a day to lie about on the grass, tell filthy jokes and drink bootleg cider. We were oblivious to those flinging themselves or some object into the air, those who grazed their knees or snapped their ankles.

There was the long jump, high jump, triple jump, shot, discus and javelin throwing. Danny was entered for just about all these and of course all the track events, relays too. I wished I could excel in something like he did.

I was tired in the morning after I had done all that Maths, or rather the maths my father had done. Maths was first on Monday as usual and to my embarrassment I got nearly a hundred per cent. I hoped the teacher would not ask how I always got my homework right but never my classwork. He probably guessed though.

I had been worrying so much about Maths that I had forgotten everything else. I was looking through my History book during afternoon tutor group when I saw 'Hadrian's Wall, Write an essay' followed by a blank page. I had not done a word.

My arm flew out to Paul beside me. 'I haven't done my homework, my History.' Jamie overheard, 'Ha, ha it's the slipper for you then,' he chortled.

'What do you want me to do about it?' said Paul.

'Let my copy yours,' I said. His eyes bulged. 'Alright,' I went on, 'Just let me have a look then, give me some ideas, I haven't got a clue what to do.'

'Why should I let you look?'

'Why not?'

'Because if you pinch my essay you'll get the same marks and I've done all the bloody work. Anyway it's cheating. And what if the teacher notices the essays are almost word for word the same?'

'We'll tell him we used the same pen.'

No dice. I pleaded, 'It won't hurt just this once will it?

Come on, be a friend?'
'Nah.'
'Jamie what about you? I let you copy my English last week didn't I, give us a break.'

Jamie laughed again the put his hands up behind his head. I thought, 'You bastard.' 'Why not?' I said.

'Because I haven't done it either,' he said and carried on laughing.

Our History teacher had always seemed a reasonable man, he did not stand for any nonsense though.

'Come in. Sit down. Hands up who has not done homework.' Just me and Jamie and another boy. 'Right, out here. Touch toes.' He was not asking for excuses. I was first. He got a plimsoll out of his top drawer and thumped it once on the top of the desk. He raised the back of my jacket and let fly. He hit me just once but I felt my whole body shake and tremble. We returned to our seats tingling. The other boy burst straight into tears, head cupped in hands. Me and Jamie were choking them back, our pride stronger.

There was a sly grin on the faces of some of the other boys. Why were they smiling? Maybe if it wasn't me it would be one of them, I thought. Competition makes you glad to see someone else given a handicap in the race. I looked at the teacher marking the homework of the others. Bastard. 'What are marks? They are nothing real, nothing you can hold in your hand, just numbers in red ink at the bottom of a page.'

I could not see that getting hit by a grown man almost twice my size could possibly do me any good. It's called assault outside the school gates. I wished they would ban it, throw away all the canes, all the slippers, all the stupid useless petty rules.

Back to school

There was a raging thunderstorm that last night of the holidays.
The rain pelted down and punched at the cracked windows
and after the frequent explosions of thunder the summer
lightening lit up the whole room, making everything like
daylight for a brief fierce second. In my bed I could hear the
dustbins rock and fall, clattering and spewing rubbish in the
front of the house. The milk bottles toppled over and I
could hear them roll slowly across the pavement to the kerb
where they smashed. The guttering around the house
overflowed, broke, and along with the slates from the roof
jumped to its doom past my window.

Downstairs, unknown to everybody in the house, water
was charging in over the back step flooding the kitchen and
ruining the carpet.

I was sweating in my bed, not with fear of the pounding
rain and vicious storm but in fear of the next day's school.
In six weeks a lot can be forgotten and a lot remembered.
Things get twisted and out of perspective. The good things
were forgotten and all I remembered were the bad things,
the bullies, the canings and the Maths I couldn't do.

Worst of all though was the thought of being split up
from my new friends in the new classes. I knew the
streaming was very rigid from now on, and I was terrified
that I would be put in a low class where everybody shouted
and had fights all day. I was equally frightened of being put
with the high class where I would not be able to do the
work. All these thoughts rolled drunk and disorderly through
my mind while the never-ending storm wreaked havoc on
the house around me.

It was a long storm but I was still awake in the morning
when its final drips plopped off the roof and the plugged
drains gurgled.

The day was a bright one, the type where the sun is in
your eyes and you cannot see where you are going. Danny
and I walked silently hands in pockets. The handle of my
bag was looped around my wrist, it was empty now like that
first day a year ago.

Things were better when I entered the playground, here
were all my half forgotten friends of the year gone. Jamie
smiled the minute he saw me.

'What have you been doing then?' I asked him.

'Sitting on me arse,' he said.

I laughed. Danny was talking to one of his friends, Joe, the son of the brickwork teacher. I thought how strange it must be to have a teacher as a father.

Here and there I spotted the new first years, very small and very nervous. This was their first day with the giants. I knew that somewhere some were being tortured by kids I knew as friends. It was our turn now. They were having bags stolen and being kicked as soon as they leaned up against the wire.

Suddenly the whistle blew and we were commanded to stand still. Mr. Price looking just the same, stood with hands high on waist.

'We've got a lot to do lads and it will be done a lot quicker with your full co-operation. We are going to organise your new classes and as the first years already know theirs they will dismiss first. Go now.' And he clapped his hands. The little boys walked out of the playground and up into the school, some of them would be the new 1M with Miss Munroe. I was jealous already.

'Good,' said Mr. Price. 'Now the second years will assemble in the north gym, the third in the south and the fourth in the main hall. The fifth and the sixth will meet me in the school library.'

So off we went. The floor of the gym was covered in a canvas cover to protect it from our dirty shoes. The whole place smelt of neglect, it had already forgotten the smell of hot stinking bodies during the holiday.

It was Mr. Joyce who took command now.

'Glad to be back at school chaps? Good,' he said without pause. 'You will line up in your last year's classes at this end of the gym and you will reassemble in your new classes at the other. What I will do is read the roll of the new classes one to six. When your name is called you will join the designated group, simple as that.'

Once we were in the old positions he proceeded with the exaggerated hand movements that were his trade mark. 'Good, I am now going to read the roll of the new class one.'

And he did. I knew damn well I would not end up there, and I didn't. In fact nobody from our group did. The top class completed, we went on to the second. This was the danger point.

'Paul Gray, Class Two.' Oh no, not Paul. I did not want to believe it at first but with just a glance to me he picked up his bag and shuffled off to join his new classmates. All of a sudden I wished they would put me in that class as well. The roll was soon finished though and we were on to the third class already. Sure enough I stayed in the third stream as I had prayed all night, although now I didn't want it. The roll of the third finished with a few of my friends standing alone with their bags. They were not going up now and knew they were going down. All they had left to worry about was how far they would drop.

Things were not so bad this morning after all. There was no assembly, Jamie was still in my class and everything took up so much time that half the morning was gone before we realised it. Next we went off to get our new timetables, the same old lessons in a different order. We would not be in the old class tutor groups anymore. From that afternoon onwards we would go to House groups. Each one contained boys from mixed years who had nothing in common except for the colour of their ties. I was in Scott-three, third rate again.

Mr. Jones stood perfectly still at the head of the class. 'Come on now boys,' he said 'I know it's the first day of term and you are all annoyed at being back, well so am I and we'll have to face up to it. So let's have a little hush and get down to some work.'

'Balls,' came the solution from the back.

'Who said that?' yelled Jonesy losing all composition, 'Who said that?' The class was in a mild state of uproar, nobody was listening to Jonesy and everybody was talking. Jonesy was a student Geography teacher we had sized up last term. It was a shame really because he was a reasonable and sympathetic man. We found that out because of the talks we had out of lesson times. Most of the older teachers, for whom we kept quiet, cut themselves off from us outside and did not even try to communicate.

Poor Jonesy was at the end of his tether, he gritted his teeth, ran his trembling Welsh fingers through his dark curly hair and left the room. Silence.

'Where's 'e gone?' someone said.

The door was left wide open and in the fearful quiet all we could hear were Jonesy's footsteps disappearing up the corridor. Then there was the sound of another classroom door opening and closing. A few seconds later we heard the door opening again and the sound of not just one but two sets of footsteps returning. I turned around to look at Jamie. His eyes were glued to the door.

Mr. Flicker and a smug Jonesy behind him made their entrance. Mr. Flicker was the epitome of the dickensian schoolmaster. He wore a batman type cloak at all times

concealing a partial hump on his bent wizened back. Very
Richard III. His hair, dark and sparse, shot out at all angles
around the back of his head. His lean pale face however,
stern now, told of a wry sense of humour and made me
suspect that he could be sending himself and everybody
else right up.

The total silence got quieter when he entered the room
and his own limping steps up and down the front of the class
were the only sound. In Mr. Flicker's gnarled hand was a short
bent cane strangely immitative of his index finger. When
pointed at a boy his finger would be so crooked that it would
be pointing at the boy next to the one intended.

Like a pinball Mr. Flicker finally came to rest. Laying his
cane flat on the desk he began the lecture that we all knew
was coming.

'Some of you, and a few of you particularly,' his eye
rolled around the room, 'And you know who you are, rode
a pretty high horse in the first year. You got away with a
few things that a few years ago would have been
inconceivable, you flouted rules and shirked responsibility.
You may say that at that age, you did not need or want the
responsibilities. Well may be so, maybe so.'

Mr. Flicker picked up the stick again and leaned it upright
on the table top with his hands on it. 'You are now, however,'
he boomed and made everybody jump, 'rapidly approaching
the age when you will have to accept responsibilities whether
you want them or not. It will,' he said precisely, 'be of
necessity.' He pronounced that last word breaking it up into
all the syllables possible.

'Very well, the first year was a trial run for your school
career and it mattered not half the time whether you even
bothered to turn up (now he tells us) but from now on
unless you make the most sincere effort you will drop
back in your studies until you find yourself in the fifth
year with nowhere to go. No prospect of a good job and
no point in staying on to take 'O' level examinations which
you stand no chance of passing.' He said all that very
rapidly as if we did not believe it.

All this time Jonesy stood hands behind his back behind
Mr. Flicker. He eyed us all in turn, especially Sammy
Johnson, too big to be as intelligent as he was and too
cheeky to be in a higher class.

Mr. Flicker went on talking for the rest of the lesson.
I cannot remember on which words of wisdom he
finished but it was a definite anti-climax after his brilliant
theatrical entrance. Encore! We received this same

monologue from Mr. Flicker every subsequent year.

Scott-three did not turn out to be so bad after all.
It became no longer just a symbol but a motley
collection of thin, fat, tall, black, white, and Pakistani
boys second to fifth year. It already had a reputation
as the sloppiest, laziest and daftest group in Scott House.
One of the boys who seemed to dominate S3 was Stevie
Leach. He was an unknown quantity to me but as a
classmate of Danny a year above me he was known as a
famous liar.

As the months of the second year passed I discovered that
to call Stevie Leach a liar was a great injustice. Over the
endless weeks and terms he told me tales of Hell's Angel
chums, married girlfriends in Mayfair and prostitute orgies
on the school's day trips to Bologne. No, only if the great
works of Verne and Wells can be called lies, could Stevie
Leach be called a liar.

I had fantasies too, though I did not try to make people
believe them. One of my favourite set pieces was that the
headmaster had gone loco. With a double barreled shotgun
in his hands and his office door barricaded he would be
yelling over the P.A. system 'You'll never take me alive,
do you hear me? You'll never take me alive.' The whole
school would be listening incredulously as with hideously
contorted face he would rave on, teachers panicking not
knowing what to do. 'I know you're all out to get me, but
you won't though, do you hear? HA HA HA.'

In the toilet opposite our S3 room I threw down my bag
and proceeded to wash my hands. Stevie Leach was in there
with five of his cronies around him. I dried my hands and
went over to see what was happening. They were too tall ,
I couldn't see a thing. I went and got my bag and stood on
it so that I could see over their wide shoulders. Stevie Leach
was very slowly turning over the pages of a magazine. The
pictures in the magazine were of girls in their underwear.
What struck me as funny was the obvious age of the book.
The pages were beginning to yellow and the photos were
so old-fashioned that the girl in them was probably
someone's grandmother by now, if she wasn't then. It must
have been a full minute before they noticed me.

' 'ere Mills, what you doin'?' 'Bugger off.'

'Where did you get that from?' I asked.

'Never you mind,' he said. 'Go on get out. An' if you tell
anybody about this you'll be bloody sorry.'

I picked up my bag and walked to the door.

'Family heir-loom is it?' I shouted.

'Get out.'

Our tutor master was a likeable man who although being firm, never got silly about it. In the fifteen minute tutor period we joked and laughed, played cards and hid his register. I was actually beginning to feel a part of the school, loyal. 'Perhaps,' I thought to myself, 'School is not so bad after all. I'm bigger now at least and there are less years above me. I suppose it must get better all the time. By the time I reached the top there would not be anybody above me to bully me or tell me what to do at all.'

Games

That public school ideal 'A healthy body and a healthy mind'
was another bee in the school's comprehensive bonnet. But
they had decided that two periods of P.E. and an afternoon
of games was enough for the body part of it — plus all the
help medical science could give us of course.

Every year for the first three years we had a medical
examination in which our eyes, ears and mouths were
checked for typhoid, whooping cough, tetanus, diptheria
and polio. It was a brief but thorough examination
culminating in that final embarrassing 'cough'.

The second year however threatened extras in the form of
T.B. injections. There were two injections starting with one
to discover if you needed the other. The first was a minor
affair which caused a little bump to appear briefly on the
forearm. The actual T.B. needle itself, the older boys told
us, was a horrendous instrument of torture. It was by all
accounts a long spike with a little spiked wheel around it.
When the spike was jabbed into your arm the smaller spikes
made contact and then, controlled like an egg whisk, the
wheel revolved and burrowed a circular bloody moat around
the central spike.

Lining up for this, boys passed out, turned a milky white
and if of a religious nature prayed. None of the rumours were
true of course, it was a clean painless jab. I had not believed
the stories anyway — much.

It was like checking the health of the man to be hanged.
It was all to make sure that we would survive the onslaught
of the 'Games' they were to bombard us with.

Immediately after tutor group on alternative Thursdays
we bundled into a coach outside the school and set off for
Epping Lodge, a snooty sports centre which condescended
to let us run riot. In our bags we carried the prescribed kit,
all washed, scrubbed and ironed by our mothers the night
before: white vest and shorts, socks, plimsoles and towel.

In the summer, games provided a pleasant interlude away
from school. Come the winter however we saw the snow
white streets on the journey and knew it was useless even
hoping for a bit of sunshine. It was too late for that.
Instead we would wish for an arctic snowflood inches thick
covering up the playing fields so that 'Games' would be
abandoned. But it never happened. Come sleet, hail and
thunderstorms we still had to take off our clothes and run

about outside. Jamie, Paul and I always did the same sports together. We played tennis in the first, football in the second and even had a go at archery and shinty. Shinty is the game where you bash each other with wonky sticks.

I was never really good at sports. I was capable physically but I could not stand the competition. I was beginning to take an interest in art. The teacher was especially complimentary of my montages, bits and pieces cut out of magazines and stuck down again in different positions. The Art room was the only place I got to see the posh Sunday Colour Supplements — we only had the Sunday Mirror at home. I spent half the lesson reading them. Just lately they all seemed full of a new model called Twiggy, a right skinny bird but I thought her lovely. Jamie said he preferred big tits.

If I was not very good at games generally I was terrible at football. I could run and pass but spent the whole game avoiding the ball because I could not tackle and was frightened of being laughed at. I was always last to be picked for teams and was the booby prize for whichever team got me. It was in the last five minutes of the last game I ever played that I got my triumph and revenge.

The team I was in scored such a disputed goal that the P.E. master let the opposing team choose who they wanted of our team to take the penalty. Of course they chose me.

Paul lined up the ball for me in front of the goal and the two teams stood away from its mouth while I prepared myself. I checked for wind direction, ground condition and reviewed the situation. Everybody's eyes were on me and everything went very quiet. Behind the goal, getting smaller all the time, I could see the other groups returning to the showers. I knew this kick would be the last, on this we either won or drew.

'Now should I place it in the top of the net where this giant goalkeeper might get at it or should I try to trick him by making it look like I was going to kick it one way and then kick it the other ...... ' The hell with it, I just booted it. The ball soared higher than I had ever kicked it before and entered the goal in the top right hand corner. The goalie made a dive for it but didn't stand a chance.

There was a moment's silence while everybody's mind flipped back a bit to verify that they had really seen me score. Action-Replay.

'Yea that showed 'em,' came Jamie's exhilarated cry from behind, and he was on the other side. It was a nice end to my soccer career and rather than return to the obscurity of left-back I decided to take up cross-country running.

I enjoyed cross-country running. I was not part of a team and even in the crowd I could feel alone. There was not the competition either: if some loonies wanted to get back first panting and wheezing then that was up to them. I just liked running through the mud and getting soaked in the inevitable monsoon. When Mr. Joyce took us he made running through the black puddles compulsory.

Epping Forest was where we ran. It was close to the Sports Centre and teachers were posted along the route to make sure we did not get lost. That was what they were supposed to do anyway. It was one week close to Christmas that this theory fell to the ground.

The grey snow was pushed up sparingly in the gutters and was almost non-existent in the darkness of the forest. Instead, icy mud hid beneath an eerie light mist. All other sports were off today. Mr. Joyce told us cross-country would keep us warm. No football because we would ruin the ground, no tennis because the courts were waterlogged, no archery because if we stood still that long we would freeze and no shinty in case we snapped each other's limbs off.

So off we went. The crowd soon broke up into fractions and got narrower all the way up to the forest. Paul darted out ahead and I stayed with Jamie. Conversation while running was almost impossible, we only managed to get out a word every few minutes. I had a stitch in my side before we even left the lodge. With sweat thick on our foreheads, our steamy breath was the only reminder of how cold it was.

A lot of the time in this part of the forest the pale moss - green trees meet the earth in a murky leaf-green bog. We passed the P.E. master, running on the spot, and were still in sight of the other boys when I ran into one of these bogs. The mud was so thick that it ripped my plimsoll off my foot and gulped it up. Knobbled.

I found it by burrowing elbow deep down and clawing it up to the surface. I washed it in an equally filthy puddle of mud and put it back on. 'O.K.' I said to Jamie, 'let's go and find the others. I hope we haven't lost them.'

'Don't panic. This is a short cut, I know this neck of the woods like the back of me 'and'. Neither of us was wearing socks and our shins were scratched and cut by the spiteful bracken. I was really worried now. We had not seen anyone for about thirty minutes. Suddenly we were out of the wood and looking both ways down a lonely path. Nothing.

'Never been 'ere before,' said Jamie. 'I'll tell you what,

let's run along it for a while.'

'You're a fine one,' I said. 'I thought you knew this part of the forest.'

'I didn't say that.'

'Like the back of your hand.'

A very tweedy woman in glasses and a hat was coming towards us being led by a huge dalmation dog. 'Enjoying yourselves?' she asked cheerily as we passed her.

'Bollocks,' said Jamie.

So there we were, our hearts pumping and stuck in the middle of nowhere on a sub-zero day with nothing on but vest and shorts. When darkness fell we were, to say the least, worried.

'You hear about things like this,' I said, 'people who get lost in the forest and are never seen again.'

'What do you think happened to 'em?' said Jamie, eyes slowly looking from side to side.

'Maybe they get kidnapped,' I told him. Jamie looked at me to see if I was trying to scare him. Everything was very silent and very dark. It was not all that late really but at that time of year five o'clock looks much the same as midnight. Then, a light. The light came from a house which became two houses and then a street. There were women doing their last bit of shopping and kids from other schools on their way home.

'Where the hell are we now?' said Jamie.

'I dunno do I?' I shouted. 'You're the bleeding walking A to Z.'

We both imagined the rest of the boys back home by now, the Sports Centre empty and the coaches gone and none of them knowing about us lost here. I imagined my mother looking at the clock and my dinner cold on the table. 'We'll carry on up this road, maybe we'll see somewhere we can recognise or a bus we can catch.'

'A bleedin' bus,' cried Jamie, 'a bus, how can we get on a bus covered in shit, an' with no money either.'

I looked down at my body. We were filthy alright. In the passing shop windows I could see my face was black. We were certainly getting some funny looks from the passers by. Just then a Mini Minor pulled up at the kerb. The window wound down and a face popped out.

'I say chaps, lost?'

We stood still and just looked at him. He was short haired and big, his posh accent didn't really seem to match his burly appearance. He must have sensed our apprehension. 'It's alright. I'm from the Sports Centre. You're the East

Road School fellows aren't you?'

'Effingham Road,' we corrected him.

'Of course, of course. That's what I meant,' he said. 'Jump in.'

Jamie hobbled to the car and put his hand on the back door handle. 'Hey hang about' I said. 'Don't forget what I told you about kidnappings. He did get the name of the school wrong didn't he?'

The cold wet street who knows where or the back of a cosy car and a free ride?

'Nah,' Jamie said, 'don't worry, I recognise him from the Centre, come on.' He opened the door and we both got in the back seat, dried mud flaking off everywhere. The car started up and sped off into the dark, the man saying nothing but seemingly looking at us every now and then in the rear view mirror. Car lights, shop lights and people outside were another land, we were in the burly man's land here. I supposed the cat had had my dinner by now. 'Y'know' whispered Jamie to me, 'he's not the bloke I thought he was at all.'

Very soon though we were driving through the gates of the gates of the centre and all of the driver's slimy and insane features vanished. Aching and exhausted we got out of the car, straight into the wrath of Mr. Joyce.

'Where have you been, you idiots?' he said, 'and where are the others?'

'Others?' we echoed.

'These were the only ones I found old man,' said the burly driver, sticking his head out of the window. A few cleaning women were looking at us and talking to each other. 'Poor little sods,' said one of them.

Mr. Joyce led us to the changing rooms. 'Look,' he said and flung the door wide open. There, on the hooks and benches were clothes, satchels, trousers and thick woolly jumpers.

'All of 'em lost?' asked Jamie in disbelief.

'About half of them anyway,' said Mr. Joyce. 'Most kept close in tow of the masters as you should have done and were back ages ago. They have already gone home in one of the coaches. We were at least confident that you had all got lost together but now it looks as if we shall be here all night rounding you up in dribs and drabs.'

He had spoken too soon. His last words were drowned out by the 'search party' coach pulling up outside. All at once boys were coming into the dressing room, arms dangling, arch backed and drooping. They were found along a stretch of road miles in the opposite direction from us.

The hiss of the shower taps had never sounded so welcoming. Naked except for the dirt we ran the gauntlet of the scalding jets of water. It ran down over our heads pushing the hair down into our eyes, past our blank chests, through the sprouting hairs on our legs and out between our toes. Everywhere dirty water was flowing into drains. I turned my face upwards and just let it pour down, sprinkling my face with a spiteful sting. Boys were sliding from one end of the shower room to the other on their backsides and others played with the heat controls. One minute we would be screaming that it was too hot and the next making a quick getaway from the icy rain.

Our bodies tingling, we rubbed well down with our towels and even felt pleasure in buttoning our tight white collars. Boys, three at a time, were combing their wet hair in the long mirror, a small boy at the front, a taller boy behind him and a taller boy still, who was Sammy Johnson, behind him.

There was just time before the cafeteria closed to have a glass of orange juice and a cheese roll and then we all flopped back into the remaining coach.

I sat next to Paul who told me his story and we both lied that we had not been scared. On the way home we looked out as usual for the St. Cilla's Convent girls. From the safety of the coach we shouted things to them and they said things to each other and giggled. No doubt what they were saying to each other was a great deal ruder than what we were yelling.

I never enjoyed games so much again. Enjoy it? Yeah, I loved it, a real adventure in a straight backed school tie world. After all, it's an odd boy who doesn't like sport!

On the wall

Another year, another holiday. All the eagerness, all the
tense impatience for the sound of those final pips on that
last day of term disappeared when they finally sounded.
We had all the time in the world. We strolled around the
corridors looking for friends and even said adieu to a few
teachers. Hands in pockets we spoke to them almost as
equals, an experience we would not experience full time
until we reached the sixth form, and even then only with
certain teachers.

The walk home too in the stifling heat was a leisurely
meander rather than the sprint we usually took it at. Things
started to look different again: the trees, the hedgerows and
litter-strewn streets started to look free again. I wondered
what it must be like to walk out of those gates for the last
time, walk out and never go back. I wondered if it would be
happy or sad, apprehensive or confident, brave or afraid.
'I'll be a third year next time I walk down this road,' I
thought. 'Wonder what new problems I'll face then;
I wonder if my spots will be gone.'

I had already said goodbye to Paul and Jamie. I would not
be seeing them at all over the next six weeks, they were just
'schoolfriends', not like Danny and Christaki. I would be
seeing them soon enough I figured, after all we had all the
time in the world. We had days ahead of us when we
wouldn't have to get out of bed until twelve but would
because you don't feel tired when the day's your own,
do you? We had days of wandering in the park chatting to
girls. Days of going far away from London and getting lost
and long rainy days of going to museums and cinemas or just
staying at home and playing records full blast and annoying
the old lady next door.

It was raining the first day of the holiday of course and
the second and third. On the fourth day however the clouds
relented and drew apart like the bedroom curtains and the
sun played on the wet pavements. Under the new blue skies
and rainbows we slowly emerged from our house to assemble
with Christaki by his wall. Washing was being put out on rope
lines, old men ventured to the pub for the first time in three
days and the oil in the road turned the same colours as the
rainbow.

Danny started to explain why it happened but nobody was
interested.

'What shall we do today?' I said.

'I think today,' said Christaki, 'we should plan the rest of the holiday.'

'Agreed,' said Danny. 'We don't want to sit on this bloody wall like last year do we?'

We all nodded in agreement and began to think.

We did not leave Hackney the whole of that holiday but played football daily over the common, a scrappy patch of muddy grass with a railway line running through it. We took on all comers, any mob of boys who thought they stood a chance against the 'Hackney Hawks'. We usually won because of Danny's rather tempermental skill. If the opposition, usually nicknamed 'Spurs', got a goal in he would get so angry he would score one immediately, singlehanded. What with that and one or two from the rest of us we usually won something like 20-17, by that time it was too dark to carry on.

It was one of Christaki's kicks that sent the Woolworth's ball over the railway fence, tumbling down the embankment and right on the glinting railway tracks. Before we could stop him, Christaki's little eight year old brother struggled under the useless mesh fence and climbed down to the tracks. Cool as a cucumber he walked onto the tracks, picked up the ball and looked into the tunnels either side to see if anything was coming. Standing there he looked up to us shouting boys and grinned one of his cheeky grins. A few seconds later the midday train shot through the tunnel fast as a bullet and was gone again in the other tunnel; but by that time little Jimmy was safely back with us playing with the rescued football.

Somedays we would play hide and seek, great mammoth games with absolutely no boundaries. Sometimes the night came and we went home without ever finding the hider. Most of all, though, we found ourselves sitting on the wall after all. Danny would kick a tennis ball about while me and Christaki discussed how we could join the American Space Programme.

On one such occasion a gang of five or six boys gathered opposite us at the corner of the street. They were poorly dressed and one or two had ugly cropped hair. The boy in front was black and wheeled a rusty decrepit old bike alongside him. Neither Danny or me liked the look of them. They approached us slowly and, we thought, arrogantly. It was high noon. The street was empty and silent save for the whining bicycle wheels. They were almost on top of us when the black boy's face burst into a wide grin.

'Hi Christaki,' he yelled.

They turned out to be some of Christaki's classmates and for an hour or two we flicked picture cards against the wall, played lolly sticks and Paddy, the black boy, showed us his penknife. As I watched them disappear up the dusky road I noted that they seemed just a bit more rough and urchin-like than most of the boys at Effingham Road School. I began to wonder if there was an unofficial grading of schools. You know, all comprehensive schools are equal but some are more equal than others. The five boys disappeared round the corner and I thought nothing more about it.

Sometimes we stayed on the wall until late in the summer evenings. Nowhere to go and nothing to do, Danny would still attempt some floodlight football under the lamp post and me and Christaki would still be talking about the moon and stars. Joe came around only rarely on his bike. He would tell us how he had just had row with his Dad and had come out for some fresh air. We did not discover until much later just how bad these rows were.

One day he came on foot. 'Some thieving git has nicked the wheels from me bike,' he told us. It was hard to suppress a laugh and impossible the next week when, once again, on foot he came to see us. 'I thought you were getting some new wheels in the week?' said Christaki. 'I did,' said Joe, 'but when I got back with 'em they'd nicked the frame.'

On the weekends we never saw him. He helped his father at work. His father was our bricklaying teacher at school and did work on building sites on Saturday. Joe said it was the only time they ever got on well together.

For all this time, all these weeks of sitting on the wall, we were watched over like a guardian angel by Christaki's grandmother. Every hour of the day she sat watching the street from her top window. She was very old and draped in the traditional black costume of old Greek women. She smiled at us English boys whenever she saw us but never understood a word we said. In her eyes, quietly surveying the Hackney rooftops, was the hope of once more seeing Cypriot hills and crystal blue seas. When, one morning, Christaki told us she had died, we could not really feel upset. It was as if she had faded into death rather than gone suddenly. On leaving her white walled Cyprus home she had already departed from the life she had always known. The mindless chaos of London must have seemed to her a sort of living death.

The six weeks passed slowly and it was so hot that at times I imagined that this is what life in India would be like.

Just sitting on a wall with nothing to do except look at my own languid shadow. Sometimes I went off to the park by myself, found a secluded patch and lay flat on the hot grass, blades tickling my ears. With eyes shut against the sun I would feel my thoughts and senses retreating into the deepest part of my mind. When the eventual human voice made its appearance it sounded like a sound never before heard.

'Mills, Mills you stupid boy,' yelled the teacher, 'dreaming about your holidays are you? What's the matter, six weeks not long enough for you. Concentrate now.' I pulled myself up in my chair and looked at the blackboard. We were a week into the new term but I still couldn't adjust to being back. The third year was going to be a long one.

It was early in my third year that we first heard talk of a swimming pool. When the Headmaster got it into his head that we should have our own swimming pool it got into everybody's head, or rather it was forced in because it was decided that it should be us that built it.

There was a small gap between the gyms and the outer school wall so that's where we put it. 'Why shouldn't we build it ourselves?' I could imagine the Headmaster saying in his cosy room. 'We have the joint experience and skill of the whole technical staff in the fields of metalwork, engineering, carpentry and building and also the manpower of the pupils.' And why not? If the Egyptians could jibe, cajole and whip a crowd of dumb slaves into building the pyramids then surely the staff could encourage us to build one swimming pool.

So over a few months which stretched to a year the structure developed brick by brick. Mr. Price wrote about it. Mr. Joyce took photos of it and Mr. Copeland filmed it. We even had a special assembly for it when halfway through the construction the Headmaster announced that some thieving buggers had stolen the lead off its roof and that we would now have to use something cheaper and not as good.

The swimming pool was made on the cheap alright. Everybody had a bash, the pupils as well as every single teacher from the technical block. We never saw our Metalwork teacher once that year. Instead of the normal lessons we were told that today our theory would be put into practice on the pool. The lower classes in each year were sometimes kept on the fetching and carrying of bricks and mortar for a whole afternoon, foregoing other lessons. I don't remember that happening to Class 1.

Our Brickwork teacher Mr. Blackwell, Joe's dad, would take a few of us to the site and tell us to take it easy. We sat and talked and he gave us cigarettes. I used to go and buy them for him. Woodbine. He denied ever offering cigs. to boys when Joe cornered him with it. Mr. Blackwell was better to other kids than he was to his own. We knew that, because Joe had told us on the wall that summer.

He was a small wrinkled man with a Bradford accent so strong that it was almost unintelligible to our East End ears. He was not a proper teacher, it seemed to us anyway. He got the job through an advertisement in the 'Hackney Gazette'. He did however give the most striking answer in reply to a question on his motives for teaching. His lessons were always informal and involved an enormous amount of backchat and, on our part, the running down of Bradford F.C. It was Jamie, trowel in hand, who asked:

'Why d'yer do it? Why do you teach in this place? I bet you could get a much better screw in a building site somewhere.'

Mr. Blackwell was silent for a moment then said,

'Well someone's got to do it, haven't they?'

Every lesson when we were not on the site we would receive our old trowels and have a sort around the yard behind the bikesheds picking out the dirty used bricks we thought suitable. We would then mix up our own cement and build a corner of wall. Every week we built that same corner of wall and broke it down again at the end. Mr. Blackwell was always complimentary and gave us marks out of ten. He helped the boys who couldn't do it, despite his lack of tolerance towards his own son. That was the other side of Mr. Blackwell.

One night, late, when Joe boarded a bus he heard a woman shouting upstairs, 'You disgusting bastard.' When he got up there he discovered it was the conductress shouting at Mr. Blackwell, dead drunk and puking over the back seats.

At other times in a rage, not necessarily a drunken one, he would throw Joe out of the house. The arguments were vicious and he would tell Joe never to come back. More than a few times Joe had to sleep the night on a park bench. Once he even called the police to have Joe thrown out, when he was still a minor. The police came and when they couldn't reason with the old man they told Joe, 'Look son, you don't have to go but why not make things easier for everyone? Go out for a few hours and walk about, then come back and see what things are like later eh?'

All that was going on and then back at school the next day Mr. Blackwell would be as nice as pie. As he might have said himself, 'There's nowt so queer as folk.'

When the swimming pool was finally finished it looked nothing like what we had expected. The dressing rooms looked like lavatories and the pool was not a ground level acre with various depths and diving boards but a massive dumpy tank which you had to climb up a ladder on the side to get into. Our newly acquired swimming instructor, blonde and bronzed, made it a rule that no trunks would be worn in the pool because fibres or material from them would clog up the drain. But in that case, why didn't we have to wear our swimming caps? And since when did swimming costumes disintegrate the minute they got wet? We had serious doubts about him.

A crash course of swimming lessons for all first years was begun and weekly, in assembly, news was given of the great breakthrough in the swimming pool. 'Sixty per cent of all the pupils in the first year can now swim.' Then seventy per cent, then eighty per cent, until in the end it was proudly announced that a staggering one hundred per cent of all first years could swim. Similar percentage announcements were not given on other school subjects like reading and writing.

Every subsequent year this astounding level was maintained and the Headmaster said that as the standard showed no sign of faltering, in a few years no boy would leave Effingham Road unable to swim. He may not have been able to write or read, but boy could he swim!

It was just a couple of days into the third term of the third year when I first met Robin Jones. I was walking home by myself because Danny was doing sports training. A couple of small boys were standing looking at a plump boy in a very clean uniform and a mass of curly hair. He was sitting on the wall of a noisy oil-floored garage and strumming furiously on a battered guitar. He was singing Bob Dylan songs at the top of his voice. Regardless of the other school kids and the horrified looks of passers-by he sang on, not just one song but one after another. I thought, 'I've got to get to know this kid.'

Teachers

Puberty is the time in life when adolescents think the whole
world is against them, and worry about acne. On Saturday
afternoons when we went to the local cinema we saw a
commercial which asked 'Do you suffer from acne?'
'I suffer from acne mate,' I called, 'I live there.'

It was no laughing matter though. Acne was a constant
source of worry. It was no consolation that Mick Jagger
looked like he had it sometimes, if he couldn't get rid of
it with all his money what chance did the rest of us have?
It was in the morning after washing my face, first in hot
water and then in cold, that they looked worst; all red
and naked. They were all I could ever see in the mirror.
No matter that ninety-five per cent of my face was clear,
all I could see were those ugly red dots.

Once in school I would give them another check and again
at lunch I would sneak off to the lavatory for another check.
They wouldn't look so bad then but they were still there,
smug and obstinate. If we ever met girls at dinnertime I would
spend a lot of the time in profile with the worst side turned
away.

Once again at home in the evening I would begin do-it-
yourself surgery. Squeezing, pinching and rubbing the spots
in flesh coloured cream, until they got so bad I would go to
sleep even more worried about them and what I would see
in the mirror the next morning.

I always wondered about that flesh coloured cream. I
imagined a black boy buying some and rubbing it on his
face and thinking, 'Huh! Why do they call this *flesh*
coloured cream, that's not the colour of my flesh!'

Another thing to worry about in adolescence is clothes.
It seemed I never had enough or good enough clothes.
I must have been better off than some boys though.
I remember seeing a Jewish classmate in his school
uniform on a Saturday and I thought 'Blimy, he must
be a swot.' It never occurred to me that it was the only
set of clothes his parents could afford. Some boys never
came in uniform at all but a rag bag of plimsolls, jeans,
T-shirts and hand-me-down jackets.

I always had to wear clothes in conjunction with each
other, wear certain clothes with certain other clothes.
For instance, I would open my cupboard and after
picking up the boots, socks and books which fell out,

I would think: 'Well now, I can't wear black trousers
with the high boots because the trousers are a bit short
and people would say, 'Have your boots had a barney
with your trousers?'

I could wear the flat shoes with the black trousers but
thought that my blazer was too long and it would look like
I had short legs. Maybe if I wore the high boots and the long
dark grey trousers that would work. But what to wear on
top?! I couldn't wear the white shirt without the jumper
because the sleeve was frayed. The shirt needed cufflinks
too. But if I wore the jumper to hide the frayed sleeve
they wouldn't see the cufflinks.

It was all too much. On top of all this I could not master
the Windsor knot, so I had to have a thin knot which
revealed I had no top buttons on any of my shirts. My mother
was forever sewing them on but the moment I did them up they
popped off. Then somedays I would be halfway to school
before I realised that I had the flat shoes on, the high
trousers and white socks so that it looked like I had two
glow-worms entwined around both my ankles. The black
kids of course, a lot of them, had trousers three inches above
the ankle. It was something we laughed about then but
eventually it became a fashion.

I looked at myself in the passing shop windows and tried to
stop bouncing. A few hairs at the back of my head would be
jumping up and down and I was afraid people would laugh.
Looking at my blazer breast pocket I promised myself I
would take the school badge off soon. All the boys, well
some, a few anyway, Robin Jones didn't wear it anymore.
'How can I convince mum nobody wears school badges
anymore?' Also I thought I must get a pair of bell-bottoms
and fitted shirts, mine all looked like I hired them from
Rent-a-Tent.

Clothes, spots, hair that won't stick down, getting
embarrassed in front of girls, hating being seen out with
parents, a world and a half against you. Adolescence.

'Y'know,' I said, 'the reason it seems the whole world
is against us is because the whole world *is* against us.'

I was speaking to Robin Jones, the guitarist. We were
walking along under Big Ben. There was a beautiful blue
sky as realistic as a colour slide and girls in mini skirts were
everywhere. London was swinging, but not for us. We were
on a school outing. It was 1967. We had come back to
school as fourth years, different people to those who had
left it the term before, or so we thought. We looked pretty
much the same except that we had grown our hair a bit

longer. Long hair meant never having to wash your neck again. But there was another thing, we had been sold on Flower Power.

That afternoon Robin explained to me that the lyrics to 'Mr. Tambourine Man' were not about a busker but a drug pusher, that Dylan was not a hack songwriter of the 'moon and June' variety, but a poet and a commentator. Robin quoted a few more lyrics to me and as soon as I got home I started to write a poem as well ......

A few lines and then I stopped. The euphoria of that revealing afternoon in the clean Westminster streets had worn off. 'Well what am I going to do with this anyway?' I thought. 'Just shove it in the drawer and forget about it, I s'pose.' The idea in my mind originally was that I would give it to Robin Jones to write a tune to. Then I I pictured him calling it rubbish, or even worse just smiling weakly, taking it and saying, 'Sure Rog, it's great, I'll do something about it sometime,' and then seeing him folding it up in his pocket never to read it again.

I picked up the scrap of paper I had written the words on, put it between the leaves of a book and shoved it in the drawer.

All the teachers in the school, young or old, came in for Pablo's wickedly funny impersonations. Pablo Angelo was a short stocky Italian boy, incredibly hairy and the best impressionist I ever saw. To know Pablo was to know every member of the staff. A few members of the younger staff once caught him doing Mr. Joyce. They made him do his entire repertoire and then applauded him for it.

Pablo was obsessed by Elvis Presley, Dean Martin, Clint Eastwood and Italian westerns. His entire record collection consisted of western movie themes. He did his homework to 'The Magnificent Seven'. Once in an English exercise the teacher told us to invent a film or write our own screenplay. Our efforts were uniformly dull and were rewarded with uniformly dull comments and marking. Pablo got top marks and was ordered to read his scenario aloud to the class. The teacher was blissfully unaware that Pablo had rewritten, almost shot for shot, 'For a few dollars more.'

He was ruthless in his impersonation of Mr. Copeland or 'The Jailer' as Pablo called him because of his need to carry a bunch of rattling keys about with him all day in his hand. 'The Jailer' was quite an imitator himself. He was an unrelated twin of Mr. Joyce. He aped him in hairstyle, dress and speech. Mr. Joyce was an ace photographer, so 'The

Jailer' became a photographer. Every detail of Mr. Joyce's life was shadowed by 'The Jailer'.

My favourite was our stand-in English teacher, a little Welshman, who told us the same two jokes every time he had us. 'Did you hear the one about the man who was so thin that he only had one pinstripe on his suit?' and 'Did you hear the one about the boy who could not stop talking? They had injected him with a gramophone needle by mistake.'

He used to read the 'Rhyme of the Ancient Mariner' like he was on stage at the Old Vic, clumping around the room with his arms flaying wildly and almost frothing at the mouth.

And then of course there was the 'Professor', a tall Scot, remarkably fit for what must have been his seventy odd years. Pablo could do him. We had the Professor for fill-in lessons as well. He told us about how in his younger days he had been a rampant Socialist and had incited miners to strike. He was a brilliant orator and had once worked up the crowd into such a frenzy with descriptions of the decadent upper classes that one of the miners leapt up onto the platform crying, 'Give me a gun and I'll go and get them.'

He had written several books, had been on Hitler's death list for when the Nazis took over Britain and had met people such as Oswald Mosley. He did not cane people, he did not have to. His appearance was that of a caricature schoolmaster; stern features, stone eyes and lucifer eyebrows. His long black cape finished off the illusion with a suggestion of the vampire.

Pablo did not do a bad job on Mr. Grub either. Mr. Grub was a kindly soul of about forty who took us for plumbing. At least I think that's what he took us for since I cannot actually remember him teaching us anything. He was a worrier and a ditherer and it was these characteristics that Pablo exploited to the full. He would not use one word when he could use a book full and spoke ever so slowly.

His lessons, as did all lessons in the technical block, began with the calling of the register to make sure nobody had disappeared in the hundred yards from the main block. But that's as far as his lessons got.

'Smith.'

'Present.'

'Ah Smith. Jimmy Smith. Now let me see, you were absent last lesson.'

'No Sir.'

'I beg your pardon?'

'I wasn't absent, Sir.'

'Is this so?'

'Yes, Sir.'

'Oh, oh I see.'

And then very methodically and very neatly he would pick up his crumb of green eraser and adjust his error to meet the boy's lie.

'Thompson.'

' 'ere.'

'You were here last lesson weren't you?'

'Yea.'

'That's good,' he said, admiring the accuracy of the register. 'That is very good.'

Maybe then Mr. Grub would leave the room altogether in search of vital papers and notes which he would find the lesson impossible to continue without. He might return empty-handed or clutching a scrap of paper which he would soon disregard anyway. The roll-call could then continue or maybe even begin again.

It was not unknown for the register process to take up to forty minutes from its start to finish, dotted with witticisms, anecdotes and nervous comments. And seeing that it was Friday and assembly had already bitten a half hour chunk out of our double period, Mr. Grub would have just enough time to stare at the classroom clock in wide-eyed disbelief and proclaim, 'Is that the time?' and tell us what we would not have time to do next week. He was working and worrying on the swimming pool a lot of the time but at least he managed to turn up for the lessons. As for the Metalwork teacher — who was the Metalwork teacher?

The new Maths teacher was not as frightening as the one we had before but was he annoying. Mr. Coombs, his first term as well, was well over six feet, had light curly hair and buck teeth which extended over his bottom lip. His clothes were very old-fashioned, a double-breasted suit which was so tight it must have drawn blood, round toed shoes and 'ankle belt' trousers.

Instead of marks or comments at the bottom of our exercise book pages he would write words like Alpha, Beta and Delta. It was a system of marking conceived out of pure bloodymindedness or it was a brilliant way of breaking down the distinction between low and high marks, because none of us ever found out what the hell it all meant. Although Mr. Coombs shouted a lot and banged his fat briefcase down on the desk he could never keep us quiet. 'O.K., O.K. I've had enough,' he shouted one day in despair, 'line up at the door.' Everybody slowly assembled at the door in two rows and then Mr. Coombs commenced to

walk us up and down the stairs, the whole three floors.
We did this for about half an hour. What this odd
punishment was supposed to do to us nobody could
quite make out. Every now and then Mr. Coombs,
walking ahead of us like the Grand Old Duke of York,
looked around with an 'I bet you're suffering' look.
We weren't. As far as I was concerned it was great.
I had no need to hide my ignorance of Maths and no
opportunity of learning. Maybe he thought that if he
could tire us out enough we would not have the strength
to talk when we got back into class.

It did not work though, so he tried detention. It lasted
for twenty minutes after school. We had to sit staring at
him, not being able to get on with our homework. There was
dead silence for if we made a sound he would start the
twenty minutes all over again. For instance, after a quarter
of an hour Jamie or somebody would say something and he
would shout 'Right, the twenty minutes starts from now.'
'Oh no,' I would say and he would say, 'Right, the twenty
minutes starts from now.'

We had been there almost an hour one night when a plump
Turkish boy, new to the school and the country got up and
announced, 'I'm leaving.'

'You can't,' said Coombs.

'Hang on, you just can't walk out when you feel like it,
I'll report you to the Headmaster,' said Coombs, as the boy
approached the door. He opened it, stepped out and was
gone. We saw him out the window getting onto a bus.
Nobody said anything.

Coombs said nothing either and pretended nothing had
happened. Next one of the black boys got up, he mumbled
and left as well. Then, all the black boys left, then Frank
Long, Patrick O'Hooligan, Sammy Johnson and the Pickles
twins. All the time Coombs was telling them to sit down.
He ran out after the Pickles twins and the rest of us were
alone for ten minutes.

When he popped his head back around the door he said,
'Alright, alright get out all of you, you're all being reported
to the Headmaster tomorrow.'

'But we're still here,' shouted Jamie, 'we bloody stayed.'

'It doesn't matter,' he said, 'you're all on report.'

We never heard anything more about it.

The next weapon on Coombs armoury was a short length
of rubber tubing. With our inky, torn books in front of us,
struggling through a bit of pythagorus, we would only have
to say one word to the next boy and he would whip out the

rubber tubing and cosh us on the head with it. He would do it quite at random and truth be told it worked to a small degree. When I eventually got clobbered with it I lost all control and leapt up like a maniac, muscles tense and almost snarling. 'Fuck off,' I shouted. It was hot anyway, my collar was too tight and I could not do the work. Now my head was stinging. Afterwards, I wondered if this was the sort of intensity that violent boys lived with all the time and that's why they boil over so quickly. I was poised ready to hit him if he said or did anything, even looked at me. As usual, he pretended nothing had happened. Maybe he coshed boys a little softer though. He must have had it in his head that the tubing was nothing, that it was only what we expected. Anyway, it strengthened Coombs's authority not a bit. The boys treated it as nothing more than a mild irritant, like a fly on your shoulder.

There was something going on by the school gates.
A tall bespectacled man holding a handful of leaflets and with three student types in tow was talking to some boys. He was giving them the leaflets. As I approached them I recognised the tall man as a teacher who had taught in the school briefly last year. Before I reached the crowd I saw the Headmaster himself look pop-eyed out of his window then appear in a flash outside draped in ceremonial cloak. He made swift progress towards the gates and shoo'd the boys inside.
From where I was I could not hear much of what was being said but in the language of the diplomat the Headmaster told them to get lost. A brief argument followed but the Head's return to his office signalled the end of it. With leaflets and scarves blowing in the wind the foursome trailed off unhappily over Effingham Road Bridge which I am sure the Head wished they would fling themselves off.
Robin Jones had one of the leaflets neatly folded in his jacket pocket and later on in the R.I, class we passed it to each other. There were various paragraphs under red lettered headings such as SCHOOL — KNOW YOUR PLACE, EXPLOITATION EDUCATION and INDOCTRINATION — KIDS STUFF?
We both had our eyes on it when two fingers in a pincer like movement snatched up the piece of paper by its very corner — as if it were a snotty handkerchief. It was Mr. Harmen. Mr. Harmen was never afraid to veer from the text. He was in fact the only teacher who ever gave us

instruction on sex even though it did not figure on the
R.I. syllabus. So that day when the leaflet showed up he
pushed aside the Sermon on the Mount and decided to give
his own. He was like ancient carvings of angels and I
always imagined him in his youth belonging to the Boy
Scouts, saying grace and helping old biddies across busy
high streets. With his short straight blond hair and blue eyes
he must have been every mother's favourite. He had a pure
smooth-skinned visage and a godly row of church-white
teeth.

'I'm glad to see that some of you are taking an interest in
this,' he said returning to the front of the class. 'I am sorry
that you feel the need to study it during my lesson but
nonetheless there are a few points in it worth discussing.
I was in the prefect room a short while ago in fact and they
were laughing at it, considering it written by students older
than them who should know better. I can't think that the
new university courses are up to much.'

'Don't you think, sir, that ....' interrupted Robin.

'Silence,' Mr. Harman interrupted back. 'I mean what does
this say about half way down, "Young people leaving school
to flog their guts out for a fiver a week." I mean, nobody
flogs their guts out for a fiver a week anymore. This is pure
emotionalism, childish. "Indoctrination." That's a good one,
I can tell you for a fact that if the sort of people who write
this stuff got their way we would all be very indoctrinated
indeed. I can tell you that for a fact because I've seen what
life in Russia is like, why they've even tried to banish
religion there.'

'Religion though......' started Robin.

'Religion and the Family, the two things on which our
whole way of life is based has found its enemy in the sort
of person who gave out this trash today.'

'He was a teacher, sir,' said someone else.

'Religion,' said Robin, 'and "God Save the Queen" is
thrust down our throats just like communism and the
Russians, isn't it?'

'Of course we've got "God Save the Queen", what do you
expect? "The Red Flag" or the Soviet national anthem?'
laughed Mr. Harmen.

'But the leaflet didn't mention Russia anywhere,'
I thought, but said nothing. I thought back to the summer
and "The Times They Are A Changing" under the chimes of
Big Ben.

'Our country is a democracy, after all,' said Mr. Harmen,
'and most people are happy to serve with the Queen as our

figurehead. Of course we have a lot of unjust things in our
society, I vote for Harold Wilson myself, but then which
country doesn't. Even the Russians have unrest and they
have a lot more regimentation than over here I can tell
you.'

'Listen to this: "uniforms stifle individuality". Rubbish.
"Prefects are scaled down policemen. They prepare children
to be those who do the pushing or those who are pushed."
Can you give it credence? How long do you think people
would get away with printing this stuff anywhere but
England?' Mr. Harmen smiled wryly.

Robin Jones, his voice smaller than I had ever heard
it before, wedged its way into the defeated silence.
'Yea,' he said, 'that may well all be true, but I believe
it anyway.'

Mr. Harmen was a man of many faces, he was a fervent
anti-racislist, a believer in equal pay for women. But all
the time he talked to us he was annoyingly smug and
condescending. Another time he told us about maturity.

'Maturity,' he expounded, 'is to know your limitations.
Maturity is facing up to life as it really is and giving up
daydreams. Limits!'

'Let's face it lads,' he said, peering benignly around the
room, 'none of you are ever going to be rich and famous
and you're not going to have a wife that looks like Bridget
Bardot. When you leave this school you'll get an average
job, settle down in an average mortgaged house with an
average girl. It is from this position and with this knowledge
that you must strive to make your life as worthwhile as
possible and influence others to do so within these
boundaries.'

'Real maturity is knowing, knowing what you really want.'

What I really wanted was to be rich and famous and have a
wife that looked like Bridget Bardot.

I was incensed by Harmen's Smug Sermon and that night
I recounted to my mother what he had said, that he had
virtually told us we were going to be nobodies. Failures at
thirteen. My mother was puzzled by my attitude and was
silent for a moment.

'Well?' she said.

As proof of God's undoubted existence Mr. Harmen would
chalk up on the blackboard a list   a) creation of world
                                      b) intelligent life
                                      c) miracles
Any argument on these or any other suggestion that the
points could have come about in any way other than a wave

of God's magic wand were ridiculed as modern nonsense.

'Of course, Adam and Eve are just parables,' he conceded, but he would never explain how he knew which books of the Bible were fables and which were not.

'They have actually found ancient wooden relics in the middle-east which could conceivably have been the beams of Noah's Ark,' he told us.

Mr. Harmen was also our Sociology teacher.

At the time I was an atheist or at least I thought I was, but then again, if you think you are an atheist then you are I suppose. It was a surprise to me therefore when I was told at the end of the year that I was to receive a prize for Divinity. The thought of actually getting a prize on Prize Day was bad enough, the pomp, shaking the Mayor or whoever by the hand and getting a prize in front of all those mothers.

'I'm getting a prize,' I told Jamie, breaking the news to him as gently as possible.

'What for?' he asked looking as if I had just struck him.

'Divinity,' I replied meekly.

Whenever I told people after I always got that same disbelieving look I got from Jamie then. 'Divinity!' I could hear them thinking, 'Has Millsy gone religious or something? Gone cranky? Seen the light? Strange. Strange.'

The glittering prizes

It was in the Art room on the top floor of Effingham
Road School that I met the devil.
Art classes at Effingham Road were more than just a
lesson, they were chaos. We got through quite a few
teachers in art classes. We started off with a bearded trendy
with a multi-coloured tie, then a blonde sex bomb with
'LOVE' written on the taxi that she drove to school, and
after her an Irish navvie disguised as a woman. She used to
yell, 'Be quiet girls' when we giggled, leapt over tables and
generally went mad. 'O.K. sir', replied Jamie. In Art classes
scrawney brushes were flung dagger-like spraying paint at the
walls, water pots were drunk and boys tied in the corner.
In Mr. Cooper however we met our match.
Mr. Cooper was the opposite of the traditional art master.
He was not effete, fat or forty. He was a six foot three inch
East End skinhead in his late twenties. When he threatened
to thump us if we didn't shut up we believed him and
whenever he talked about sending us to the Headmaster,
we didn't. He was that sort of bloke.
In the summer he let us out to draw on the lawn and he
let us argue that Picasso was a wanker and that John Lennon's
lithographs were just as good anyway. Not many teachers
would have put up with that. He was a knowledgeable blues
fan, hated all the teachers in other ranks and ate just curry.
A week before prizegiving I was talking to him and the
longhaired Nick Taggert.
'I don't think the Head can be all *that* bad,' I was saying.
'I mean look at all the things you read in the newspapers
about teachers caning kids because they've got long hair.
The Head's never said anything about me.'
'Has he ever said anything to you Nick?' asked Mr. Cooper.
Nick just shook his head.
'You're lucky you don't have to worry in that direction
at all,' I said laughingly to Mr. Cooper.
'Nah,' he said. 'I never had long hair. I think it's a bit of
a bore, it's a thing of the past. The Skinheads are where
it's at now you know.'
'How d'yer mean?' I asked. Nick wrinkled his forehead.
'I mean the whole long hair thing and the hippie thing,
it's a middle class snort. All these so called freaks dropping
out, tripping out, bombing out and what'aveyou, they're
only doin' it because they know they've got a plush 'ome

to go to when they get bored. It's like all these lefty students –
they chuck Marx out the window when they leave
university and work in their dad's firm.' Mr. Cooper
indicated the rest of the class. 'Look at these kids here,
they can't decide not to work, their parents would chuck
them out of the house. No mate, the skinheads are alright,
most of 'em aren't bad lads.'

'What about all the Pakki bashers and queer bashers then?'
I said, 'at least the hippies 'ave got some new ideas, want out
of the rut we're all in. Skinheads don't have any ideas except
wanting to look like each other.'

'That's true of freaks too, isn't it?' said Mr. Cooper. 'It
was one of your longhaired blokes who said it: "Everybody in
this room is wearing a uniform." It's true in every room in
the world.' Nick grunted.

At that moment the door opened behind us and everything
went quiet. We knew who it was without having to look.
Boys stood dead still with paint on their faces and tried to
hide their pictures of opened legged ladies.

The Headmaster, smiling so we would know it was a social
call, raised a piece of paper to his glassy eyes and stayed
where he was in the doorway.

'Sorry to interrupt your teaching,' he told Mr. Cooper.
Was he being satirical? 'All I want to say is that all prizewinners in this class must assemble at breaktime in the main
hall. It's a rehearsal for next week. Something well worth
missing break for I'm sure.' No he wasn't being satirical.
'By the way,' he said pretending it was an afterthought,
'which boys here are receiving prizes?' I put my hand up.
So did Keyhole Kate, a particularly lanky boy with a huge
nose.

The Headmaster glanced briefly at Keyhole Kate and then
stared at me, his geriatric smile visibly sagging. 'Do excuse
me,' he said 'but will you turn your head around.' I squirmed
awkwardly in my seat.

'Tut, tut, I dare say you were going to anyway but will
you please make sure that you get a haircut before the
prizegiving.' He waited for a challenge but I neither showed
him two fingers nor nodded.

'Thank you,' he said stonily to my stare and was gone.
The hubbub of the rest of the boys started up again but both
Nick Taggert and Mr. Cooper just sat looking at me.

'Speak of the bloody devil,' I said.

In that week leading up to prizegiving I gave the hair
problem a lot of serious thought and worry and decided I
would not get it cut. I was getting the prize for Divinity

after all and look at the bloke it was all about.

Come the evening of the presentations though, the rebelliousness, indignation and stubbornness I had been nursing all week suddenly died. I was sitting with all the prizewinners and looking at my reflection in the window thinking 'well it doesn't look *that* long' when Keyhole Kate came in and said, 'Blimey, you haven't had your hair cut, you won't half cop it.' My nerves jangled.

'D'yer think so?' I said. 'There's blokes in the sixth getting prizes with longer hair than this.'

'You won't half cop it,' he repeated.

'Oh do shut up,' I said. 'He won't even notice me.'

'Like hell he won't, he'll have you he will.'

'Oh for Christ's sake, shut up,' I said angrily and then inspected myself in the window.

'I ain't half goin' to cop it,' I said.

Minutes before going down to the hall I was frantically experimenting in the sink. With flat palm and comb I was trying to flatten my hair against my head and trying to discover some way of tucking it into itself so it would look shorter. All I succeeded in doing was making it look like I had been stood out in the rain.

All the prizewinners took up the first three rows on the left side of the hall. I was in the second and spent all the time positioning my head directly behind the boy in front hoping I would not be seen by the Head. The stage itself was a riot of flowers, pretty colourful tulips shooting up and pale hanging weedy things. I had never seen the hall like this before.

First the teachers and their wives took the stage, then came the people nobody had ever seen before: officials, women in funny hats and the like. Then the Deputy Head, the Head and the guest of honour. The National Anthem by the school band plus kettle drums and Mr. Price on violin had us all on our feet, but almost at once the Headmaster seated us with a discreet gesture of his hand.

First off was the chairman of the Board of Governors, so it was said in the programme. Next were the speeches of welcome by the monitors and prefects and then the Headmaster's report. He gave a glowing report of the school and especially the swimming pool. He made no mention of the raincoat stealing ring that had been stealing from the cloakrooms. I lost a brand new mac that way. I was not paying much attention and was feeling a bit jittery. I tentatively raised my hand to my head occasionally to flatten my hair.

The next item was billed in the programme as Presentation of Prizes and Address by T.F. Selby C.B.E., PhD., B. Eng., C. Eng., F.I.E.E., A.M.I., Mech. E. So this was it.

We had already rehearsed it all. When the applause for the boy before you died down, you had to get up, walk to the stage steps, wait for your name to be announced, then go up. We were to shake hands and receive our prize, a book, from the guest, walk on a few steps and on the mark of a painted white dot, take a bow to the audience.

Prizes for English first: upper middle then lower school then the others. Lenny, Jamie's little brother, was getting a Geography prize. He was a lean boy with a very short styled haircut. It seemed to be a fast emerging fashion. He was grinning all over his face when he got up. He waited at the bottom of the stairs for his name to be called. CRASH. Lenny fell flat on his face on the stairs. There were some giggles from the boys. But undaunted and still smiling, Lenny walked very straight backed across the stage. He was looking outward all the time, looking for his mum. His huge boots clump clump clumped louder than mallet blows. He received his book, shook the guest's hand and then clump clump clump, bowed and clump clump clumped off the stage.

What was supposed to happen now was that he should walk through the thin passage under the stage and up into the gym next door from where we were to file back into the hall and our seats. We heard Lenny go all the way underneath and saw him reappear at the back of the stage behind the staff. He had come up the wrong stairs. The Headmaster saw him out of the corner of his eye and made as discreet gestures as possible indicating that Lenny should get lost. Lenny's smile disappeared and so did he. 'You don't think anybody noticed, do you?' he said to the boy next to him when he got back.

There were only the Music prizes to go now and it would be my turn. I made last minute adjustments to my hair. I was sweating, and my collar and tie were too tight.

"Now the school prizes for Divinity," I heard someone say, and then in no time at all 'Roger Mills'. I was already in the right position. I looked straight ahead of me at the brown wooden steps. I felt assured anyway that I could not make a bigger mess of it than Lenny. I started to ascend the steps and thought how little the space was between the guests' feet and the rows of tulips.

'Thank you very much,' I said. Too soon though, the guest was just picking my book off the table. I had picked

a thin illustrated book called 'The Story of Newspapers'.
The guest was looking at the cover and inside it. 'I'm in a bit
of a muddle here,' he said. 'We've lost the slip with the name
on it. I think this is the right one.' I could see it was the
right one but didn't like to say so. 'Here you are,' he said
at last, 'it must be the right one.' I took the book with one
hand and weakly shook his hand with the other. Now all
that was left was the bow and remember not to come up
at the rear of the stage like a pantomime devil. Where's
the bloody white spot? I had no trouble finding it in
rehearsal. I could not find it and just bowed where I was,
still edging left and right looking for it. There were more
titters from the front but they were fortunately drowned
out by the applause. Mum and Dad were out there somewhere.

When I got back to my seat Keyhole Kate behind me
leaned forward just a little to say, 'Cor, you should have
seen the Head looking at your hair when you were waiting
at the bottom of the stairs. If looks could kill ......'

We were still only halfway through the awards. There
were prizes for Art, Economics, Natural Sciences and a good
half-dozen others. There was a Governors' Prize, something
called an Old Hexonians Endeavour Award, a Headmaster's
Prize for each house and finally it was all over. The final
applause and song of praise was as refreshing as the hiss
of a newly opened lemonade bottle.

'I wouldn't be surprised if the Headmaster called you to
his office tomorrow,' said Keyhole Kate. 'He weren't half
giving you filthy looks.' But I didn't care anymore. I told
Kate to shut his face and found my parents. Everybody was
getting their coats on.

'That chap spoke to you much longer than anyone else,'
said my mother. 'He was a real educated man you know,
have you seen all those letters after his name in the
programme. What did he say to you?'

'Oh nothing much mum,' I told her.

'Don't be modest,' she said. 'What did he say?'

'Oh he just said how interesting the book looked and
asked me if I wanted to be a journalist.' I told her that
to keep her happy.

I walked along with them, my book under arm. I saw
Jamie but without his parents. He hadn't got a prize.
We smiled and nodded to each other but didn't say the
things we wanted to say to each other, not with parents
about.

My dad put his scarf and cap on and said, 'I told you
this was a good school, mother, they've got a band.'

Aggro

Almost overnight it seemed teenagers everywhere were
going bald. Kids who for the past three years had been
chastized for their long flowing locks were turning up to
school with their hair so closely cropped that you could see
their skulls. They were chastized for this as well.

They had a completely new style of clothes too. Heavy
brown boots, sometimes steel toed, sta-press trousers and
Jeans with turn-ups. Their shirts were button-collared Ben
Shermans with braces, regulation red, and maybe a Cromby
jacket. It was an ugly fashion, the perfect camouflage for
the brick streets they lived in. It was a style so frighteningly
close to army uniform that it made you wonder if the people
were right who said all kids really wanted was a spell in the
army.

The skinheads were attacking on all fronts.

Breaktime. Friday. Under the stairs.

The dirt stained coffee machine rumbled, belched and
threw out a splash of coffee. Had the cup been released
from its hatch it would have been Keyhole Kate's. 'Blow
this,' said Kate under his breath but undaunted tried again
and was rewarded with a cup of black coffee, half full.

A mob of skinheads had been watching the performance
and clapped politely. 'Thank Gawd for that,' said their
leader. 'I bin getting awful thirsty over 'ere.' All the boys
leaned away from the wall and walked slowly up to Kate.

'Be a good kid and give us yer drink will yer?' he said.
'I'm gasping.'

'Why should I?' said Kate. 'I paid for it, didn't I?'

' 'Cause I wan' it, that's why you should give it to me. The
other reason being that if you don't I shall punch your
'ead in.'

Another boy in the group moved impatiently about on
his feet. 'Come on Dave, don't let's stay 'ere, you dunno
who'll come down the stairs.'

'Shut up Rick,' said the leader. 'I'll give you some bovver
an' all if you don't.' He did not look away from Kate's face,
just kept 'screwing' him.

Keyhole Kate, braver than he had a right to be, raised the
cup to his lips and took a sip. The skinhead's face erupted,
teeth bared, cheeks bloated like a toad and forehead coming
down like a landslide. A fist was held up to Kate's face and

almost immediately turned into a solitary index finger. Very slowly he pointed the plump finger at his own head. It was a moon shaped object with a fat piggy face beneath it. His rusty hair was barely visible, like lonely tufts of grass on a muddy football pitch.

'You see this?' he said grabbing Kate's shirt with the other hand, 'you see this, it means something y'know. It means something.'

There was a real anger in the skinhead. Real violence. It was all so logical, the Long Arm Law. This boy was a skinhead, skinheads are tough and therefore Kate must surrender his cup. Kate, shaking now, handed it over and the skinhead drunk it down in one before he let go of Kate.

' 'Ere come on. Leave 'im alone Dave. He is in a year above us after all. Let's go for a smoke behind the bike sheds.' The boys half pulled, half followed the affronted skinhead to the bikesheds.

Kate wiped the sweat from his forehead and adjusted his shirt front. Surely the most patient of them all, he decided on just one more try at getting a cup of coffee. A coin appeared in his hand and he fed it into the machine. The machine gulped, laughed, mumbled and once again threw the cupless coffee into its full swill dish.

Dinnertime. Monday. Outside the cake shop opposite the school.

Stevie Leach spotted a tall girl, walking across the road. 'I used to go out with her,' he told the little boy with him. 'I blew her out though, she couldn't stand the pace.'

They came into the cake shop where I was standing in the queue and Stevie nodded to me cockily. Stevie was lining up when the girl entered the shop behind him. 'Hey Stevie,' said the little boy and tugged at Stevie's blazer. 'That's the girl you used to go out with.'

'Shut up Shrimp,' said Stevie under his breath.

'Ain't you gonna say hello to her Stevie?'

'Shut your bleedin' face,' said Stevie, face turned away.

'Two egg and tomato rolls please,' he said to the assistant.

'Wait your turn sonny.'

'Hey Stevie that is the girl innit, the one you used to go out with?'

'For Christ's sake shut up. Ain't them rolls ready yet, Miss?'

'Wait your turn.'

Once he had his rolls Stevie turned in such a way that he would not have to look at the girl.

'Why didn't you say hello to her Stevie?' said the little

boy outside. Stevie said nothing. 'Y'know, I don't reckon you used to go out with her at all.' Stevie turned around to face the little boy. 'Now listen 'ere .....'

At that moment a rusty blue mini van came flying round the corner fast. It screeched past Stevie Leach and a crowd of school boys and went to make off down Effingham Road. The window was wound down and from inside a bag of chips, cold and stale, came hurtling out. It was never known if it was aimed or if things like this are decided by some higher authority. The open bag of chips made direct hard splattering contact with Stevie Leach's face. Vinegar, salt and all the rest of it smack dab between the eyes. The little boy said nothing, fearing his next word could be his last.

In Stevie Leach's mind there was nothing else he could possibly do. He chased the van. Effingham Road is long and straight and he could see the van was quite a way off. Stevie never actually meant to catch it, of course. He was like a barking dog kept safe from conflict by the tight tug of his master's lead: if he thought there was any chance of catching the van he'd have stood holding the chips.

As he ran, though, the van began to slow down. As it did, so did Stevie. From outside the cake shop we saw the procession of the van and Stevie getting slower and slower. He was still trying to look like he was going fast, but virtually running on the spot.

He reached the van eventually, but what to do then?

The back doors opened a fraction, just enough to let out a fist. The fist, large and ringed, executed a tidy punch to Stevie's lower jaw. The fist disappared, the doors neatly shut again and the van was gone.

'I've got your number, you lot," he shouted, hand on jaw. 'I'm gonna get the 'ells Angels on to you, d'you hear?'

Midday Monday. Around and in the school.

Nobody knew Nick Taggert much. Nick hardly said anything to anyone. He was very tall, had very long hair and a face that betrayed no emotion, happy or sad. He had suspicious deep-set eyes and thick stubborn lips. He was not a fan of the Beatles or the Stones as most of us were then but of the big soul singers of the time, people like Otis Redding or Wilson Pickett. The only time I remember him taking any interest in the classroom was when he pleaded with the Music teacher to play a record he had with him of the emerging Jimi Hendrix. The teacher put the record on but took it off again even before the intro had finished and the voice came in.

Nick always dressed smart himself like his soul idols, flashy suits and flairs and lots of cheap rings. He was not a bully — he was not that extrovert and was not known for violence. But there was always something about him that kept the wary at bay.

Nick wanted to leave school as soon as possible, which was about the middle of the fourth form then. In his last few weeks at Effingham Road he was rude and contemptuous to the teachers and let it be known what he thought of the characters who were always criticizing his hair.

His taunts and grunts culminated in a fist fight with Mr. Coombes. Mr. Coombes, who had even given up rubber tubing by then, ordered Nick out of the room and made the fatal mistake of pushing him along when he did not think Nick was going fast enough. Nick took a swing at him and caught him around the head. Coombes tried to get in a bear hug and they both engaged in a clumsy wrestling match all the way out of the door. Very soon Coombes staggered back in, hair awry, straightening his clothes and checking for blood on the side of his head.

We thought Nick must have gone home as he usually did when he was sent outside, but to our surprise we kept seeing him throughout the day. Like a suffering ghost he kept appearing at the little glass window of whatever room we were in.

We had Music on Monday, and he still had a score to settle with the Music teacher. Remember?

Nick must have seen the teacher leave the room for a while — we were listening to a classical record he had left on. Nick burst in with two other dubious gents he had collected during the day. He took a flick knife out of his pocket and with a 'click', started to destroy the revolving disc of black plastic. He gouged at it, scratched it and stabbed it, the deck bouncing up and down and the arm bouncing. We sat attentively and watched him as if it was a demonstration of a new art form. Nick and his accomplices departed, to leave the Music teacher to puzzle for the rest of his days how the record, once so fine and clear, now sounded like someone sawing wood.

Nick did leave as soon as possible. Indeed, he didn't have much choice. But it was only a week before he returned, like the convict from 'Great Expectations'. He loomed up again in the little window and at lesson change we talked. After years and years of displaying his long dark locks to the teachers' annoyance, he had now completely cropped it in the current idiom. He told us that day that he was due to appear in court the following week.

I followed his developing career in the Hackney Gazette court reports. Each time his crime escalated and the sentence got stiffer.

Very recently I saw him again, but I didn't recognise him at first. He recognised me though and we talked while I waited for a bus. His long hair was back but now he sported a few facial scars, a set of broken teeth and junkie eyes. He wore an untidy pair of trousers and a torn shirt. Gone were the smart cut jacket and flares and he had no rings. He was wearing plimsolls now, not cuban heels.

'Where have you been?' I asked.

'For the past twelve months,' he replied, 'I've been in stir.'

'A year?' I queried. 'Something serious?'

'They thought so,' he said.

The bus came then and I got on saying good-bye to Nick. 'Must have been serious to get a year,' I thought, but I had not asked what it was. I just didn't want to know, didn't want to know the person Nick had become.

Late afternoon on a hot Friday. The lecture theatre.

Biology film it was. It was in the seconds when the film flicks off the spool that a fight broke out in the back row. The lights clicked on and the two boys, still and as silent as statues sat staring at each other eyeball to eyeball. A twitch or a blink a declaration of war. Their bodies were hot and taut and poised for action. The animal scent of aggression could almost be seen rising from their bodies. They were like two alley cats beside a bin which only contained enough food for one. One boy was black and the other white.

'Dear oh dear, oh dear, oh dear,' said Mr. Copeland, the 'Jailer' Is it you again Jarvis?', completely ignoring the white boy.

'What's it all about this time? Jarvis said something unintelligible, held his damp brow and looked straight at

'What?' Mr. Copeland said.

Jarvis said nothing, stared back at him and did not move a muscle. Mr. Copeland stared back at him for a few seconds then turned his back. He walked back to his own desk and threw the register he had in his hand onto the polished top. He put both hands up under his jacket at the small of his back and resumed his staring competition with Jarvis. The rest of us were silent, eyes rolling from side to side to each of the contestants. It was the Jailer who broke the silence.

'It's always the same isn't it? You are always the first to baulk when you get told off for it. And you always accuse me of victimization. I'll tell you laddie there's no boy in this school victimized, white, black, yellow or green, but I'll be damned if you'll receive special treatment for it either. You must realise, Jarvis, that it is not colour that gets you into trouble but your attitude.'

'It's because of my colour,' Jarvis mumbled.

'What?' said Mr. Copeland. 'What?'

Mr. Copeland sighed and sat back on his stool. 'You must understand that in a school where the coloured boys are in the minority, in a school where there is any minority, then that minority will be instantly noticeable and when they do anything wrong or step out of line the majority will say, "Look, that's the coloured boys for you," or "Look, that's the Greeks for you," or whoever. It is a hard fact of life and it is for that reason that you must be a sort of ambassador for your race. You must be on your best behaviour and show your critics that whatever they say is not true.'

Jarvis did not fancy the ambassador's job and wondered why he could not act like everybody else, just because of his colour. He looked more pained than ever now, his conflict with the other boy over, forgotten in the midst of the Jailer's preaching.

'And it's no good sitting there trying to look like a martyr. Martyrs traditionally have causes and I don't see yours laddie.'

If Mr. Copeland meant that then he must have been blind.

The lights were turned out again, the projector started to hum and vibrate and the screen was a square of light. I could still see Jarvis's eyes in the dark, still staring straight ahead.

Wednesday. Fifth of November. Stoke Newington High Street.

The air smelt different on Guy Fawkes night, and not just at night. All day from the minute I got up it smelt of Golden Rain, Box o'Tricks, Silver Arrows and another thousand volcano, oblong and aeroplane shaped fireworks all looking like irregular Christmas parcels primed to explode in your hand. The smell that seemed to hang in the air most though was of those smokey bonfires and the sacrificed guy.

A mid-day sprinkle of rain disappeared by lunch and in the afternoon we silently prayed it wouldn't return. It did of course. Teachers jumped on the bandwagon and told us in the science rooms why a Jack in the Box shoots up, why a Catherine Wheel spins and why a Jumping Jack chases you all around the garden.

The Geography lesson was about how the Chinese

invented gunpowder and Mr. Davies, our History teacher, told us his theory about how the gunpowder plot was cooked up by the government of the time. He said that Mr. Fawkes was framed in order to bring the Catholics of the country into disrepute.

At the end of the day though all we were worried about was 'Light the blue touchpaper and stand well back.' How many of us tomorrow would have bandaged fingers, singed hair and no eyebrows?

Danny and I were walking along Stoke Newington High Street, bags full of fireworks. 'Penny for the guy, Mister?' said a little boy. I gave him a tanner–a Mister already! Looking back I saw two skinheads approach the boys and the scruffy guy. They kicked its head off. 'Violent sods,' I said to Danny. Violence? I didn't know what violence meant.

Another evening in Stoke Newington High Street. This is the first of those Out of School "educational experiences' I mentioned in the introduction. It happened two years after leaving Effingham Road. 1973.

It was a dark part of the High Street, but still a High Street. I saw them from a long way off and they called to me as I was walking past them. 'Hello there m'boy d'yer think yer cood spare some cigs?' Scots. 'Sorry, don't smoke' I told him.

The larger of the two men, curly haired and with a moustache, lumbered in front of me. 'D'yer have any money?'

I had already made my first mistake of the evening: I didn't run. I just quickened my pace and hoped the smaller of the two would restrain his friend.

'Don't mind him, boy,' he said, 'he's pissed.'

Quite suddenly my arms were clamped down tight by my sides in a bear hug from the small cheerful Scot. I was trapped on the inside of the pavement and was ruthlessly shoved into a dark shop doorway. I didn't have the use of my arms but I could have kicked I suppose. I didn't fight though. A mistake. I might have made things worse for myself but oh how much better I would have felt later on in my recollections of the incident.

I was given a cruel punch to the jaw before formalities were exchanged. My glasses flew away. 'Give us yer money,' they commanded, 'an' we don't want pennies.'

'I ain't got nothing,' I told them, 'leave me alone.'

I was lying, it was my third mistake. More batterings to my face confirmed my suspicions that I had a lot more to lose than money.

'Fucking hell,' I shouted, 'here you are this is all I've got, a quid.' I was telling the truth now, I plunged my hand into my pocket and got out the crumpled note. Greedy fingers snatched the pound and experienced hands frisked my wrists, shoes and fingers for jewellery or hidden loot.

It was now I made my most stupid mistake of all: I attempted to reason with them, attempted to reason with two heads of bone hardened as sorry children in their rough city. They were playing the game as taught to them.

'I'm only poor, why me?'

It was an attempt at some sort of working class unity. They made it clear with a barrage of insults they weren't interested. They tore a chain and cross from my neck. I tried to break loose now, enraged, but only got another punch in the mouth.

Shock was wearing off now and I was beginning to think. I feared a spiteful punch to the stomach. I had seen what it had done to others, seen others on their knees with water running from their eyes. I dropped to the floor. I was still making mistakes though. Now they were kicking me in the body and the head. My bloody sticky cheek touched the ground to pick up a layer of dirt and I let out a groan. 'Let's go,' I heard. Not words of sympathy but of wariness. They had been there too long.

It was the last words I ever heard from the muggers' lips. They were never caught.

I lay motionless on the cold floor. No one came. There were people almost opposite at a bus stop. Did they see what happened? Could they have seen what happened and yet done nothing? Anyway, why should they care? It's just another mugging. They were catching the last bus home to their own problems.

I raised my head and put a hand to my outsize face. I felt around for my broken glasses then stood up. What now? Partly due to school you get addicted to instructions, what did I think would happen when I went to the police station. Would they tell them off. You're on your own out there. It's the place to go though isn't it? Someone must hear about this.

The sergeant at the desk was casual and critical.

'So you were mugged you say. Were they black?'

'No.'

'And so you didn't know your assailants?'

A ride in the police van was provided free of charge. Three policemen and me were hoping to spot the fleeing thieves. All we saw were the inhabitants of a Stoke Newington Saturday night: plenty of drunks, lean black youths standing talking on corners and frail old men in cloth caps walking

unsteadily home. 'Don't worry son,' said the policeman in
the seat next to the driver. 'If we get 'em in the back
'ere we'll give them a good going over.' Good.

After our fruitless journey we returned to the police
station. We were waylaid just once. A Pakistani shopkeeper
had had his front windows smashed. Particulars of my
muggers were taken: Descriptions, time, what was taken.

'You sure you don't want to go to hospital?'

'Sure.'

'Want a lift home?'

'No thanks, I only live across the High Street.' What can
happen to you in the High Street?

'Hello mum, hello dad, I just got mugged.' 'Oh about five
hundred yards down the road.' 'Yes I've been to the police.'
My parents were horrified. What kind of area is this now
anyway, they didn't bring up their son to be rolled around on
the ground by two drunken Celts. They talked and fussed a lot
but I didn't want to listen. I just wanted to wash and go to
bed, I didn't sleep though.

I spent all the next day quietly. All day going over the
incident in my mind, imagining what I might have done and
what I should have done. I started to get sharp headaches that
made me clutch my head and roll on the bed. I decided to go
to the hospital after all and they took X rays. No injuries,
nothing visible.

A young policeman, cheerful and friendly visited me and
with understanding tones took a statement. It was the last I
heard of it.

Now I knew what violence was.

Bunking off

I was behind in a lot of things at school—bunking off was one
of them. One of the reasons I never bunked off until the
Fourth Year was that I never realised how easy it was. All
you had to do was go to tutor group, morning and afternoon,
and be registered and then walk out of the back gate. Not
always though: a register was taken at the beginning of all
the technical lessons, so you had to be there. Also if you had
Mr. Price you stayed as well. If he saw somebody was missing
he wouldn't accept, ' 'e's sick,' as evidence. He would check
up with the tutor register to see if you had been there, and
if he found out you were playing truant ......

Boys would spend their days at Clissold Park or in the
Effingham Road Cinema, a small flea pit which showed
films like 'Seven Slaves against Rome' and 'Hercules versus
the Moon Men', all in gaudy colour, all Italian and all
atrociously dubbed.

If their mothers worked, some boys went home with
friends and some boys just walked the streets, going around
Woolworths, having a tea in the Wimpy Bar and watching
out for over-zealous policemen who might want to take them
back to school.

One boy, a curly haired Maltese, was away so much and for
so many months at a time that Mr. Jones said he had to
reintroduce himself every time he came back. Another boy
who made his entrance mid-term we found out to have been
at Borstal. He was a stocky boy with an expressionless face
which eyed the world with fear and suspicion. His every
movement was slow and calculated as if he were constantly
under suveillance. He hardly ever said a word and certainly
never started a conversation. Very soon he too took to
spending his afternoons away from school.

The Headmaster told us frequently from the assembly stage
that these boys, and the latecomers, and the ones who did not
wear school uniforms, and those who didn't do their
homework were the ones doomed to a life of poverty and
obscurity. No employer would put up with what he had to,
he told us, not when they were paying you.

That Autumn, a few days before the end of term, Paul and
me heard they were setting up a fair at Millfields. We figured
it would be a nice way to spend an afternoon. So instead of
returning to school after lunch we walked up to Millfields.
It was, to our disappointment, half-assembled: a half dozen

or so major attractions surrounded by Roll-a-Penny, Hoop-la and hot-dog stalls.

The bright lights, which were all we had seen as children, could not hide the dirt and rust that covered everything now, couldn't hide the tarnished chipped red paint on the 'Rocket to Mars'. The clanking and whining of the heavy capsules as we spun endlessly into space were a greater cause for anxiety than any strange planets we might visit. A rainy day previously had given the ground a fresh shape: ditches and mounds appeared where they had not existed before. The whole area was carpeted in brown leaves and where it wasn't we almost left our shoes in the mud. The chilly wind blew down our collars, not helping a bit. The people who worked the machines sat about swearing and the teddy boys who took our 1/6d for the rides looked put out by our presence. 'Gi'us yer money, I ain't got all day.'

HA HA HAAAAAAAGH! The ghost train roared into action. It was three minutes of black canvas, a luminous skeleton and somebody still building it inside. The electric shrieks and yells gave us no shocks but when the train smashed through the exit door, the daylight almost blinded us.

A dirty tent housed the fruit machines, pinball wizards stood menacingly about and played table-football. The large ringing dinging and bleeping machines looked out of place on the wet grass. Their home was Soho with a dog-ended floor beneath them. Comic Italian types with prehistoric Tony Curtis hairstyles and wide shoulders gave Paul and me the feeling we had stumbled in on a late 1950s British comedy film. Greasers, rockers and Teds abounded here among the bouncing spinning contraptions. Here they could risk life and limb and impress their girls. It was like Southend, a last resort.

Paul decided he would like to shoot some tin ducks and he won a key ring. I rolled pennies into somebody's pocket and we both froze at the top of a big wheel.

'Could you imagine being stuck out here all night?'

'We'd freeze to death.'

'Yea, but can you imagine if we didn't freeze to death and were stuck up here all night?'

'We'd freeze to death.'

The skinheads were more in evidence as it got later and Paul and me decided we would soon go. But first there were just two more things to do. We just had to go on the Rota-Rola and then see the Cornish Pixie.

'Roll up, roll up! You're just in time for the event of a

lifetime. Come and see the Cornish Pixie. It is said that
anybody lucky enough to see a Cornish Pixie will have good
luck for the whole year. There is nothing here to insult your
intelligence. What you will see is not a boy but a thirty-two
year old man, the smallest you have ever seen, a real Cornish
Pixie!' said the voice through a loud speaker. We figured
out it would be a plastic gnome, but we just had to see it.
It was only 4d.

First though we went to the Rota-Rola. Paul had been on
one before in Brighton. They were huge cylindrical things
he said where twenty or thirty people stood on a ledge on the
inner side of the cylinder. It begins to spin around and when
it's going fast enough the ledge disappears and everybody's
left hanging on the walls like flies. No danger of falling off
at all.

We paid our money to an uninterested lady who gave me
the wrong change and we went in. It was like a big barrel with
a tyre in the middle. There wasn't room in there for half a
dozen people, let alone thirty and instead of a ledge to stand
on that's what the bald tyre was for. We waited a few
seconds in a noisy silence and then with a rude jolt the
barrel began to spin. Everything turned on its side, my
stomach tried to make an exit out of my mouth and I made
an impulsive embarrassing grab for Paul's hand. His cheek
was pinned to the side of the barrel and he yelled, 'I think
my neck's broken.'

In less civilized times this revolving mindkiller would have
been a torture — now we paid for it. I started to slowly slide
down the side and that's how I knew it was slowing down.
I prayed a silent prayer and it was answered. The bloody
thing stopped. We both fell out of the Rolo feeling very,
very sick. Paul was still worried about his neck. 'That was
terrible,' he said. 'I had my face against the wall, and when
I tried to straighten it and look ahead it got pushed down
the other side.' He continued to manipulate and put his
head through a series of exercises so that he knew it was
still connected to his head. I had to sit down.

'Come and see the Cornish Pixie. Come and see the Cornish
Pixie. Once inside he will start talking to you and shake your
children by the hand. Don't forget also to ask for a lucky
bean which he will give you free of charge. You won't find a
pot of gold inside but merely by seeing him you will have
luck the whole year through. You'll find nothing here to
insult your intelligence, no trickery. You will see a real
Cornish Pixie. Hurry, hurry, hurry, you're just in time.'

It was getting dark and we were beginning to get bored,

hungry too. I thought of home and the warm cosy kitchen. We began to wonder as well whether we had been missed at school, and whether we should have stayed after all.

The lights were bright, yellow and red against the grubby skyline. The yells and screams of young girls were all over the place and long queues stood in front of the candy floss stall which was a van and no doubt doubled as an ice-cream van in the not long gone summer months. We began to recognise other boys from school, but they were dressed in their cheap suits and had girls with them, simpering and grinning and clinging to their arms.

A few drunks were hanging about in groups among the kiddies' merry-go-round and Helter-Skelter. There were parents too, with their kids ragged and in awe of the goings on around them.

'We'll go now shall we Paul?' I said.

'We've got to see the Cornish Pixie yet,' he protested, 'we've just got to.'

'Bloody plastic gnome it'll be,' I said and we laughed.

'Here you will see something you will remember for the rest of your lives. You will want to tell your friends about it and when you do they will want to come and see it as well. This is the only chance you will ever have to see a real live breathing Cornish Pixie. Hurry. hurry! You're only just in time.'

There were a couple of girls in front of us in the Pixie queue but we were both still in our school uniforms and felt we had no right to claim them. We pretended to each other that it wasn't us they were turning round to and giggling about.

The thud of dodgems behind us and the yelling of the greasers couldn't drown out the insistent drone coming out of the tinny speaker by our ears.

'Roll up, roll up you're just in time for the event of a lifetime. Come and see the Cornish Pixie. Once inside he will start talking to you and will shake your children's hand. Don't forget to ask for your lucky bean. It is said in Cornwall that if you see a real Cornish Pixie you will have luck the whole year through ......'

We paid our 4d and followed the queue which trailed around the outside of an imitation garden fence. It was brightly lit and had fake green grass. A real Disney type place. In the centre was a little garden wall with money surrounding it where people had missed. Maybe that's a Cornish Pixie. There was a little sign on it about it being a wishing well but I didn't get time to read it because I spied something out of

the corner of my eye. It was a midget. He was dressed in a
little red suit and hood. He was very small: the smallest I
had ever seen. I hurried by without getting my lucky bean,
not looking at his face. Outside I didn't look at Paul's
face either. We stood around as if we weren't leaving and
felt embarrassed, more for the little man in the red suit than
anybody. What a way to have to make a living.

'I wish it had been a plastic gnome,' I said.

'Let's go home,' said Paul. 'It made me feel sick, the
Rota-Rola I mean.'

'What else?' I said.

Assemblies

Anyone who was late for school in the mornings was sent straight to the Headmaster. In theory anyway; A fast agile pupil running at full pelt could dodge past teachers and prefects alike and lose himself in the crowds milling about the playground. It was better to go the whole hog. A few minutes or half an hour late and you stood a good chance of being caught. An hour or two hours late and you could walk in unbothered, unquestioned by anyone.

It was normal for latecomers to be ordered to run through the playground again and again for as many times as the teacher thought necessary before proceeding to classes. In winter this mild punishment took on a vaguely sadistic undertone. In the really cold snowy months the playground was transformed into a solid sheet of ice.

The victims would go through one by one and would either give a stunning display of gymnastic type balance and remain on their feet or go flying and crashing over in hilarious fashion while we cheered and guffawed from the windows. We laid bets on who would stay on their feet the longest. It was Effingham Road's own ice spectacular.

Most of the latecomers were in before assembly, which we went to directly from tutor groups. On particularly sunny days in the summer months, assemblies were held in the playground with us on foot and the Headmaster on box with microphone.

Usually, through the week assemblies for the separate houses were held in the gyms and on Friday a full assembly in the main hall. In we would all march as the school band played hymns, and either find a seat or, if unlucky, have to stand at the back or lean against the walls. Most teachers sat on the stage in front of the sixth formers. Some were strategically positioned around the hall ready at a whisper's notice to grab offending parties and haul them off to await a beating.

The Headmaster would arrive with a flurry of black cloaks. The hall's side doors would be flung open and, preceded by the Deputy Head, the man himself would enter: a bald, bespectacled man in his sixties who, when he smiled, used only half his mouth. The hall was always in reverent silence when he entered, partly I suspect because we had been kept waiting for so long that we had run out of things to say. The band with their battered instruments had long ceased playing by now, doubtless due to the lack of breath and affrontery. They all sat in a semi-circle, heads bowed in front of the stage like dusty monks waiting to be nudged into chant.

Christianity is about love, but I don't remember the Headmaster encouraging any talk about that. After all it was an all-boys school. No, the Headmaster saw the Bible stories as nothing more than aids to school discipline and would usually relate apocalyptic Biblical events to a school incident involving vandalism of desks or some such thing.

At the entrance end of the hall, long, dowdy curtains covered the tall windows. They were never quite drawn and in the hot weather the sun shone through and aimed a solitary spotlight directly on the Headmaster's head which beamed like a halo.

There was not a large amount of religion talked about in those Friday assemblies. But we did sing, the teachers mostly, and we did pray. I did too, except in later years when I held my head high defiantly above the sea of scruffy bowed heads despite the Deputy Head's warnings.

I had always thought that Britain was not really Christian but still pagan. All that Jesus had done was to join our already long list of ancient gods who ruled England with rough justice for thousands of years before his birth at Bethlehem. Evil doers perished and the good were watched over by the even more ruthless. Even today it seems to me the idea of a strong but just attitude makes more sense to people than trying to love someone who is out to hurt, murder or exploit them. Mr. Harmen himself, the R.I. teacher, was forever smashing kids in the face with the blackboard dusters and bits of chalk that he flung with an unholy accuracy.

And yet every morning for five years the forelock tugging of religious ceremony was forced upon us. Besides prayers however, assemblies were an excuse for self-congratulation. Sports events were duly recounted and endless rows of boys shuffled about embarrassed on the stage receiving handshakes and certificates. Danny always got rewards for running while he was there but when he left he lost interest. Running did not fit in with his life anymore. You could not do a hard day's work, have four pints and beer in the lunch-hour and still expect to be the third fastest sprinter in London as he once was. Various members of staff came up and gave information about various school activities. One teacher, the swimming instructor, made a cabaret of it with jokes and props like a loud winding watch.

The Deputy Headmaster, a man destined to remain

deputy Headmaster while all about him rose or fell not necessarily depending on their merits, was an old man who moved about cagily on the balls of his feet. He was left with all the mundane announcements nobody else wanted to make. By the time he finished we were all daydreaming, minds far above the hall, the minutes dragging by crippled.

Even Old Boys of years past were introduced as being fine examples of our education system. They had joined colleges and universities and even attained degrees. 'You don't get degrees through sitting on street corners and protesting, you know lads,' the Head said on one such occasion. Two young teachers exchanged sardonic glances over my head.

Every now and then the Head would decide our hymn singing needed looking into. 'That was a sorry sound,' he would say suddenly out of the blue. 'We are all, not just the staff, all going to sing that again.' Indeed, up there on the stage it was like the finale of the Gang Show. English, Scottish and Welsh teachers' voices rang out with the glory of God. Like the Sally Army or 'Stars on Sunday' choir they raised the roof while us boys murmured and whined our way through it all. I only opened my mouth to talk to Jamie or Paul. In the end though we would all sing and would not be allowed to go until we enjoyed it. The only hymn I managed to raise any steam over was the one with all the 'Praise Him, Praise Hims' in it.

Sometimes the whole assembly seemed to be held in honour of a Class One boy in my year called Alistair Aron, a curious, saintly-looking boy who received prizes and commendation almost every week. Anything you were good at, you could guarantee Alistair was better. He was tops in English, Maths, Geography, History, Music and French, but above all this he was well liked for he was no swot. He was a good mechanic and all round sportsman. The Headmaster would talk glowingly of his achievements in the chess club and the debating society and so many other activities that we wondered how he ever found time for it all. Alistair Aron was destined to be the school's Head Boy and surely its finest scholar in a university career.

It was in an assembly that we were told of his death.

There was a lot of hub-bub and talk on that morning. Rumours abounded and much speculation was given to reason why a full assembly was being held on a Wednesday. Some boys knew already but only half believed it. The hall was hushed and for once the Headmaster was not smiling or pompous as he spoke to us.

'Alistair Aron is dead,' said the Headmaster. 'Alistair Aron of 4I, whom I'm sure you all knew either by sight, or personally, is dead.' Silence.

'When I heard of Alistair's death I asked his mother to come and see us,' he continued, 'I suppose to console her. She's in my office now waiting to see me in a few minutes time and I still have no idea what I shall say to her.'

Until now the Headmaster had stood erect in the centre of the stage but now as if relieved at having made the initial announcement he leaned back on the table top.

'Alistair Aron was an exceptional boy. An intelligent and honest boy. He had a worthwhile, very worthwhile future ahead of him. His enthusiasm and perseverence were astounding. He always strived for the top and more often than not he got there. Why only last prizegiving he was put forward for no less than five prizes. Five.' Then he added with an ironic laugh, 'I even asked him to accept just one so that we had some left for the other boys.'

Only very slowly the Headmaster's words, unusually slow and deliberate infiltrated our minds. We would never see Alistair again maybe save for a faded school photograph. The Headmaster's words faded into the background like in a bad film when the vivid memories creep into the conscious and along with a hundred piece orchestra blot everything else out.

'Even though Alistair was an intelligent boy,' the Head was saying, 'he was just a boy like the rest of you. And any, any one of you torn so hastily from life is a loss, a great loss.' He was looking at his feet.

The assembly parted in silence save for the sound of rain starting to spit at the glass of the windows. The whole school shuffled off to their classes in heavy melancholy. I was upset. We never did discover the cause or reasons for Alistair's death and we never tried to find out. He was dead and that's all there was to it. Just one possibility lingered in the mind, but no, not Alistair. If he had found no reason for it all, with his potential, what chance for the rest of the Effingham boys?

His parents came about a month later to witness the planting of a tree in Alistair's honour. We of his year were led out and stood on the lawn. We listened to the traffic while the Head and Alistair's father shovelled a token heap of earth while the mother looked on. It was a touching sight but afterwards there was nothing. It was all too frightening to think about.

A short while afterwards in the hot summer of 1969 there was another death of another young man, and another assembly. The man was a blonde musician who had drowned in his own swimming pool under the influence of drugs, legal drugs, to help his asthma. This time though, the death was reported nationally on TV and in the press. The man was Brian Jones and the assembly was the Rolling Stones free concert in Hyde Park just three days after.

Hyde Park looked medieval with young people drawn from all over England garbed in brightly coloured clothes and with frizzy or straight long, long hair. If it was a uniform it was a damn sight more attractive than the one for Effingham Road. People moved coolly and orderly into the park until they found the stage. A small semi-circle up front of the stage soon became a big one and I found a place with a good view and stayed there. The area was the Cockpit, a natural amphitheatre near the Septentine, so called because cock fights were held there centuries before. People had been sleeping around there all night.

I was sitting next to a hippie in red bellbottoms, beads, a large floppy hat and beard, not at all like the people I met back home.

The stage was massive. On each side of it vast towers of scaffolding held dozens of amplifiers. 'Blackhill Enterprises', the name of the organisers, flapped on a banner above the stage, a film set itself with palm trees and yet more amplifiers. Giant pictures of Brian Jones were erected and were welcomed with applause.

Someone set a large waste paper bin alight in front of me but carried it away to extinguish it without prompting or a teacher's shout. Young people here seemed adult and responsible in a way we were not allowed to be in school. Even the Hells Angels came over as saints. Lots of people were talking and singing but nobody got taken to the Headmaster's office. Radios and cassettes were playing, flags waving and people dancing. Nobody got told off.

A news broadcast was on — 'Already thousands of young people are gathered in Hyde Park and are reported to be reasonable and quiet.' At this the crowd let out a terrific yell to make up for it. The skinheads were there too, investigating. It was one o'clock and the show began. The Third Ear Band played 'Alchemical music' as their publicist put it. 'Why don't you play something we all know?' someone shouted.

The sun was scalding by the time King Crimson took the stage and people were climbing trees to get a better view. The groups passed the time: Screw, blues king Alexis Korner and his band, Family and Pete Brown's Battered Ornaments,

even more battered after a slow handclap. There was only
one group we had come to see though. We took one last
opportunity to stretch our legs and then they were on stage:
Mick Jagger, Keith Richards, Bill Wyman, Charlie Watts and
Mick Taylor the new Stone.

'Cool it and listen,' Jagger said and we did, half a million
of us. It was something by Shelley about death and read for
Brian Jones. Then the guitars and drums thumped and
screeched into life and 3,000 butterflies were released.

'Honky Tonk Woman', 'Jumping Jack Flash' and 'Love
in Vain'. 'Bust the place up Mick!' two black guys beside me
were yelling. Jagger then removed his delicate white jacket
which was a girl's dress and went straight into 'Stray Cat
Blues' all about a sixteen year old groupie; then they did
some blues by Robert Johnson. Girls clambering up onto the
stage were taken away and disposed of. The sinister song
'Gimme Shelter' was followed by the even more sinister
'Midnight Rambler' with Jagger adding emphasis to the
guitar slams by playing his heavy belt whip-like onto the
canvas.

Then he announced 'This is our only old one.' An echo
of the past few years. It was that song again,

> '...... And I'm trying to make some girl
> Who tells me
> "Baby come back maybe next week"
> Can't you see I'm on a losing streak?
> I can't get no satisfaction .....'

African drummers crowded the stage for the finale,
'Sympathy for the Devil.' Everybody was up and dancing,
some banging cola tins together. Throughout the noisy chaos
everybody seemed happy and friendly. I knew for certain
that an alternative way existed and that order did not need
a cane to be maintained.

Jagger finished dancing with a black man in a devil suit
and shouted, 'We gotta go.' He went but the tribal beating
of drums and congas went on for several minutes without him.

Then the Stones were gone. The MC called, 'It's no use
yelling for an encore I'm afraid. The Stones have already left
the park.'

And then a few minutes later,

'Could the crowds please get away from the Stones' truck
so they can leave the park.'

On the return bus ride home besides the excited energy in
me, I had underlying thoughts about all those adulating fans.

75

Was it just hero worship or was it an appreciation of their art? Did those people ever strive to add something of their own feelings? I had never taken a particular interest in English at school but I thought that maybe writing might be worth concentrating on. I had after all had a go at poetry, with the idea of Robin turning them into songs. I could not play the guitar like Robin nor even afford one. I knew I would never get a chance at directing 'Ben Hur' and the only camera I had was a Brownie. Writing though? All you needed was a biro. It was something to think about for the time being.

Task Force - softly softly ?

We were looking at a pretty girl. 'You may or may not have heard of Task Force before,' she said. She sat at the head of the class in Mr. Harmen's pulpit while he stood behind with his hands behind his back.

'That's the police init?' someone whispered at the back.

'Task Force,' continued the girl, 'was first formed in 1964 and was financed by the Ministries of Education and Health; don't let that put you off though,' she laughed lightly. 'It was made clear right from the start that there would be no members, badges or committees. It's just a purely voluntary organization for youngsters like yourselves to help and assist the aged. Now it's not as frightening as it sounds, in fact it's quite fun. What it means is a bunch of people getting together under supervision and with materials provided by us and decorating an old person's home. Believe me, wall-papering and plastering can actually be a gas. As you may have guessed by now I'm asking for as many of you as possible to lend a hand. The activities usually take place at weekends whenever you can spare the time. Over 10,000 young people are already involved in the organization helping out where they can. Decorating is not all we do, of course. Old people often need assistance writing letters, ironing, sewing, gardening, cleaning windows, repairing furniture and dozens of other little jobs we don't even think about. Even shaving can be an ordeal for some old men.'

After the woman's little speech and a few questions Mr. Harmen came out of the background and thanked her in his 'talking to civilians' voice. 'Now lads,' he said turning round to us in his teacher's voice. 'I wonder if those even remotely interested in helping could put their hands up.'

Nobody put their hands up.

'Come on now lads,' said Mr. Harmen. 'I'm sure you can do better than that, come now.'

Nobody put their hands up.

'You'll find, I think,' Mr. Harmen said to the pretty girl, 'that they are very reluctant to commit themselves to anything right out.'

'Evidently,' she said.

'The magic Christian didn't look too pleased, did he?' I said later in the playground.

'What's all that about then?' said Rosen, a sixth former we sometimes chatted to.

'Task Force, it's a voluntary ......'

'I know what it bloody well is,' he said, 'I do decorating for them myself at weekends.'

'Ain't it all a bit goody though?' said Jamie.

'You're joking,' exclaimed Rosen, 'you haven't seen all the birds from St. Cillas Convent who go in for it, helping to decorate and the like.'

On the way up from break Paul and I saw Frank Long from our class coming out of Mr. Harmen's room looking both ways.

'Where have you been?' we said.

'Oh nowhere,' said Frank, 'just seeing Harmen about something, nothing really.' He sloped off down the stairs.

Paul and me looked both ways then entered Harmen's room.

'Don't tell me,' said Harmen looking up from his desk, 'that you've changed your minds about Task Force as well. This really is marvellous, you make about half a dozen now since break who've come to put their names down.'

One morning in July a lot of us arrived at school bleary eyed and tired. I stood by our usual bin staring at Paul. He was staring at me. We both had bags at our feet and beneath our eyes and our hands in our pockets.

'You stayed up to see it then Paul?'

'Yes, did you enjoy it?'

'Enjoy it? That's a funny thing to say, like it was a musical or a show,' I said, 'I just saw it.' At this point Jamie joined us.

'Did you see it you two?' he asked.

'Yes' said Paul. 'Did you enjoy it?'

'Huh! I s'pose so. Bet it was better in colour though, sound could have been better too.'

'I waited up all night, only had an hour's sleep this morning,' said Paul.

'Of course it's all a bloody waste of time,' said Jamie, and there was a hint of devilment in his smile.

'Waste of bloody time,' exploded Paul. 'The greatest technical and scientific achievement of the human race. Millions of men, all of them scientists, a waste of time? That moon landing is the first step in our escape from this miserable planet. This place isn't going to last forever you know. What are future generations going to say when the world's all knackered and the river's full of three star. "Oh it's alright. Our dummy ancestors knew that space exploration was a waste of time." '

'And money,' said Jamie.

'I'll go along with that bit,' I said. 'There's people starving in America itself an' that's not even considering the Pakis.'

'What are you talking about?' said Paul, hands out of pockets now and arms animated. 'If they hadn't spent that money on space research you don't really think they would have given it to the poor and needy, do you? If they hadn't gone to the moon they would have poured it into developing atomic lavatories or something. I don't know about you cynics but when I saw Armstrong on the telly last night, everybody in the world watching him getting out and actually treading on the moon, a chill went up my spine.'

'Mine too,' said Jamie. 'Our storage heaters go off at midnight.'

'What was it he said?' Paul continued regardless. 'It's only a small step for me but it's a giant leap for mankind.' And then Paul's eyes lifted towards the heavens seeking the soiled moon with those great yankie footprints on it and those astronauts hopping about like giant luminous rabbits.

'I'll bet they scripted that line a few months before an' all,' I said.

'Yea, probably by the same bloke who writes John Wayne's scripts,' said Jamie winking.

We nodded and grinned at our feet. I wondered how many people had dreamed of this moment and wondered what this day would mean for mankind. Well here we were and it didn't mean a thing.

'Wasn't it this weekend you two were going to do one of them Task Force jobs?' said Jamie.

'Oh it was great,' said Paul. 'We weren't together though, I was decorating an old man's flat in Dalston.'

'And I was doing an old girl's house overlooking the Hackney Downs,' I said.

'By yourself?' joked Jamie.

'Of course not,' said Paul taking him seriously. 'There's about six of you under supervision from someone older and more experienced. If there's not enough of you or too many then there's the Area Organizer, Alex. He drives about in a Task Force van and brings lunch and moves people about if they are needed somewhere else. I was talking to him. Actually, he's communist you know?'

'No he's not,' I said, 'cos I was talking to him as well and he told me he was a Marxist.'

'Isn't that the same thing?' said Jamie.

'Is it? I don't know,' I told him.

'You weren't there all weekend were you?' asked Jamie.

'Just Saturday,' I said, 'that day we did the paintwork and

wallpapered the ceiling. What a joke that was, all coming down on me 'ead. Those who started on Friday night did all the stripping.'

'Lucky them.'

'And those who went on Sunday wallpapered, tidied up and did all the rest of it.'

'That's a lot of work to do for nothing,' said Jamie.

'I dunno,' replied Paul. 'If you had seen this old bloke. He had been in two world wars and never missed a day's work in his life and he's living in a crummy flat. It's better to decorate that up though than stick them on the top of a tower block!'

'That's progress,' said Jamie, 'like men on the moon.'

'The fellow in charge of us,' I told them, 'was a right East Ender. He said his wife is always on at him to decorate his own house but he can't get round to it because he's always doing someone else's. He's a skilled painter and decorator. He's painting up a girls' convent next week. He told me he would try and bring a dildo back next time for us to look at.'

'What's that?'

'I don't know.'

There was quite a bit of progress going on around school as well. In the administration area a beautiful scale model in a glass case showed us the projected plans. There was the school with its three blocks and right beside it in the middle of the crossroads was a gigantic round green thing. All the corners of the streets were to be cut off to make room for it.

Labourers and digging machines were already making a trench out of the school lawn. The loss of it was sadly lamented by the Headmaster and he near enough told us he thought it was a bloody awful idea as well. Where the flower beds once stood, and which was now mud, would one day be an underpass for pedestrians to cross under the new roundabout.

The noise caused by the workers and the closer traffic was being taken into consideration, they told us, and when we got back from our summer holidays the windows on the whole of that side of the building had been double glazed.

Because we could not open the windows though, they had to put in a whole new ventilation system. This took much longer and the workmen became a regular feature at the school. In dark blue overalls, with spanners hanging out here, there and everywhere, they banged and crashed huge pipes and vents into creation. All over the ceilings, walls and floors, holes appeared and other holes were filled up. We quite often had a lesson in one room while workmen laboured noisily in the next.

And in the end , when the workmen had gone and everything was clean and shining, the ventilators buzzed more noisily, rattled louder and made more racket than the traffic would ever have done.

The Task Force jobs were taking up quite a few of my weekends by now but on the weekday summer evenings me, Christaki and his little brother Dimmi still sat on the wall and Joe still made guest appearances. Only now he had grown out of push bikes and had a motor scooter.

In the dark empty mews, Christaki and Joe played 'Chicken'. Joe would mount up and start his bike at one end and hurtle towards Christaki who stood in the middle of the alley. When they were about a yard apart one of them would chicken. Either Christaki would leap out of the way to safety or Joe would swerve past him and prepare at the other end of the alley for another go. This jousting match continued for some weeks until one night came the inevitable crunch.

What was it Mr. Jones asked us in school: 'What happens when the unstoppable force meets an immovable object?' Well what does happen? We were about to find out.

With manic grin Joe, like the bolt out of a crossbow, shot towards Christaki. Full throttle, fuel pipe rattling and indicator popping out the dial, he just kept on coming. Christaki's agile torreador body shifted apprehensively on his feet. His face turned into that of a weasel's, nose sniffing the wind, eyes on the snorting machine and ears listening to the hoarse grumblings of its 100cc hulk.

After the accident we all remarked how cinematic it had been. We could almost see it in slow motion action replay. Joe's bike getting bigger and bigger and getting nearer and nearer to Christaki and both their faces showing that 'I'm not budging this time' determination. Then we saw their faces turning to 'sick in the stomach' horror as they realized they both meant it.

As if in frightening close-up we saw Christaki's grimace as he caught the machine by the handlebars and then his hand turn red as he pushed it into the headlight.

Joe flew off the bike rodeo style and fell right on Christaki. With bloody knuckles and grazed faces they rolled about on the floor for a while wondering if they would ever be able to get up again. The bike, on some unknown conquest of its own, jumped around for a bit then landed on its newly painted side with that hollow scraping sound, and with its thin splinters of glass, nuts and bolts, shooting off in all directions.

Joe got up by himself and together we all helped Christaki to his unsteady feet. He had not come out of it so well. His wrist and forearm were badly bruised and his hand was wide open with bright red blood foaming out.

He had to go to hospital but after stitches and heavy bandaging they let him go that same night. Joe and Christaki never played that game again. There was no longer any need. Besides Joe started work soon after and, like Danny, began to spend his evenings in the company of his elders in the pub. Little Dimmi and I were soon the only ones left on the wall. Everybody else was going to work. Danny had left school in a hurry, pleased to get out. He had no job though and it was only by luck his uncle managed to get him into an electrical firm where he was a foreman. Danny did not speak much about his new job and only shrugged his shoulders when asked about it. Little Dimmi and I would see him coming home in the hot sun and we would shout across the road to him. Some days he did not even acknowledge us: he would just carry on walking in his dirty working clothes, head bowed, not at all the same boy I used to go to school with. He was a worker now.

He did not come out with us much in the evenings from then on and when he did he was sullen and silent. He didn't kick the ball under the streetlamp any more.

'I'm going to the pub with Joe. Are you coming Rog?' he would say.

'No thanks, I don't think so,' was always my reply. I did not have the money and I didn't have the clothes they could afford now they were working. I just had jumpers and school trousers. One night before he went out though he stayed and talked to us by the old wall.

'Still doin' the Task Force jobs are yer?' I nodded. I was sitting down and he was standing in front of me.

'I 'ave enough work all through the week,' he continued. 'I'm knackered by the end of the day. You need a pint or two to put it all back.'

'I bet you wish you were back at school don't you?' I asked.

'Bollocks. I went back to that bloody place last week,' he told us. 'I went up to pick up me C.S.E. certificates, for all they're worth. I went in me working clothes and I was waiting outside the secretary's room when the deputy comes out. You know what he said? He said "Are you one of the men working on the roof?" I looked at him and shook my head not saying anything. "Are you one of the men working on the roof?" I ask you, all the bloody years I bin there an' he didn't even know who I was.'

Little Dimmi thought it was really funny and began to laugh.
'Bloody school, let me tell you about bloody school. They
teach you nothing. I wish I'd left the year before actually.
I didn't need any of them certificates and I'd 'ave a years
apprenticeship behind me already. As it is now I'm earning £11
a week and doing day release college just like the ones a year
younger than me. We'll all be electricians at the end of five years,
only difference being I'll be a year older than them. An' as for that
English an' stuff, just forget it. I tell you Rog, go out now and
learn a trade, the school won't do yer no good unless you want
to be a poncy bank clerk or something.' Danny was quiet for a
minute, afraid maybe he had come out of himself too much.
Indeed it was the longest speech he had made since leaving school.
   'Anyway,' he said at last, 'I'm off to the pub. You sure you
won't come along?'
   'No thanks Danny, really. Perhaps next time eh?'
   'OK,' he said, 'I'll hold you to that, the next time.'

Drinking partners

Late in the summer of my fifth term Christaki's dad decided that
he had had enough of England. He closed up his little shop and
returned to Cyprus. He took his wife with him and, of course,
Christaki and little Dimmi. The years of sitting on the wall were
suddenly over. We said our goodbyes without even shaking hands.
Too shy. Now there wasn't anyone to walk to school with, I was
alone. At first I wrote to Christaki regularly, to a funny named
town in a funny little island half way across the world. As we
realized though that we may never see each other again we slowly
dropped off corresponding.

Back at school we were half way through our C.S.E. courses,
lots of studying to do and too much homework. If I did not go out
with Danny, I thought, I would never get out in the evenings at all.

Wearing a pale green jacket that was too small for me even two
years before, shirt and black flared trousers I waited in the tube
station, Leicester Square. The whole world was going on around
me. It was Saturday night and young men and their pretty
girlfriends were everywhere. Old men, too lonely and too tired,
wandered about hollow eyed and tatty. Mercenary Northerners
looking for Tartan bitter, 'Shaft' black men and teenage hippies
were all part of the West End scene. Every now and then I would
see a man who just had to be a gangster. With his hair slicked
back, dark glasses, rings on his fingers and the whiff of 'Brut' as
he passed by, there was just no way he could be anything else.
I had come here via Soho and had played the faces game all the
way. I had been picking out the prostitutes and the strippers
from the crowd.

I was here to meet Danny, Joe and Keith. As I waited I shifted
nervously about, moving my arms which were pinched under
the armpit by the awful green jacket.

I had never met Keith before. He was a workmate of Danny who
said he was a 'good bloke'. In the time I stood waiting I paid out
about two bob to assorted winos and Scots drunks and told a
dozen foreigners 'No, I'm sorry, I'm a stranger here myself.' I also
got looks from a tall man in a red rainhat but he cleared off as
soon as Danny and the rest came up the escalators yelling and
nudging people in all directions. They were twenty-five minutes
late.

I had already started going to pubs with Danny, well one pub
to be exact. I would sneak in and sit by the wall while Danny
ordered the drinks, Light and Bitters. We went in early and it did
not occur to us to leave before it closed at eleven. It was a dismal

pub but at least it was near home. It was most frequented by
Irish and black people and a fat barman who turned the juke box
right down if we put anything 'objectionable' on.

Little boys and girls, not even ten years old, waited outside
the pub steps for their mothers and fathers to come out. Every
now and then they would take out a lemonade and tell them
they would not be long: they'd be hours. It was a scene my
parents had told me about when they had been children, waiting
all night for their parents to appear drunk and carefree in the
dark streets. I thought that had all gone now.

There were fights in the pub too, violent and nasty. Foul mouthed
scrawny women and depressing old men with whiskey jaws talked
toothlessly to each other while their wives sat in silence drinking
stout. I felt that this could be a scene from a hundred years ago
when these same people's grandfathers sat in these same pubs. I
got the feeling of never getting anywhere.

'No doubt about it,' I said to Danny once, 'if it wasn't for cheap
beer there would have been a revolution in this country years ago.'
In the warm light this side of the bar with a few pints inside him
there's not many will give a bugger for anything except who's
buying the next round.

In the West End that night though I was told we were going on a
pub crawl. It was still early and hot and sticky. People were
spilling out of the bars and the crowds only thinned out slightly
when the films started. We had a couple of drinks in two different
pubs but had to fight our way to the bar for them. A nudge, a
jostle and half of it was spilled on the floor. What to do with the
Light Ale bottle? On Keith's lead we threw them on the floor and
kicked them under the feet of the crowd. At about nine o'clock
Keith suggested that we go to a pub in Blackfriars he knew. They
played all the best sounds he said and the people were really
cool. Anything to get out of this heat.

I skipped down to the toilets in Leicester Square by myself.
I did not wash my hands, I had heard stories of people pushing
broken razor blades into the bar of soap. A loo flushed and a door
opened behind me. A young man just a few years older than me
staggered out. He was rolling down his sleeve and ran his arm
under the cold water tap. Spots of blood appeared.

'You silly young bugger,' the attendant was saying to him as I
went up the stairs. 'You silly young bugger, why d'yer bloody
do it?'

The music in the West End pubs had been so loud and the
atmosphere so chaotic that the tube ride was the first place I got
to talk to Danny's friend, Keith.

'Still at school are you?' he asked.

'Yea, fifth form, maybe I'll leave after the C.S.E's.'

'What you gonna do when you leave then?'

'Oh, I don't know really. Maybe something — no I don't know.'

'I only left last year y'know, at Easter. I didn't know what to do either but I've got a brother in the trade, so I thought why not?'

'You'd be in the fifth then? You must be the same age as me.'

There were already a few drunks about annoying people on the trains, some on the platform seats, heads down, maybe a pool of vomit beneath them.

I could not see much difference in the new pub we went to except that the music was louder and we had to fight harder to get to the bar. The place was almost in darkness except for the frequent explosions of light and colour from a distant corner. I ordered a lager here. While I was waiting for the drinks a light went on above the toilet door and a bewildered man came out to cheers from Keith and everybody else. Keith explained to me that the blokes behind the bar had rigged up the Durex machine in the lavatory so that a light went on whenever anybody put money in. I wondered if the man's girlfriend knew his intentions before. She did now.

Everybody was young here: trendies, yobos and a similar crowd to those I had been with in Hyde Park. Most people stood, but some sat at table under long snakes of smoke climbing up to the roof.

That drunken feeling. Faces smiling and a blur of coats and lights as you turn. And one thing, it might be a cigarette. smouldering in an ash tray, taking up the whole of my gaze. It was up to the others to carry me out at the end of the night. No matter how hard I focused my eyes on someone or something they would roll and sink right down until I was looking at my feet. Sitting on the tube platform listening to the girls' pissed chorus, saying goodbye to Keith, sitting in the smokers' compartment and sniffing, looking at the people looking at me on the bus, everything took so long. I started to sweat. My tight jacket had a strangle hold on me now, and every stranger's voice irritated me. My whole body shook and tingled.

'Joe, Danny, I've got to get off the bus.'

'What for?'

'I'm gonna be sick.'

'Joking?'

'Uh, uh.'

'Hey look Dan, you get off the bus with Rog. I'm already late and it's because of that all the rows start in my house.'

'O.K. Joe,' said Danny. 'Come on you.'

I was not sick but Danny and I had to walk all the rest of the way home, him propping me up. I was seen by Keyhole Kate that night and I believe I commanded a little more respect from him because of it.

Danny opened my front door for me, put the key back in my pocket and shoved me in. I hoped my parents would not guess that I had been drinking let alone drunk. I said a few words to them that sounded alright to me and left them watching the Midnight Movie. It was no good though. I even managed to get into bed and thought 'Good, that's it, now for a good night's sleep and I'll wake up feeling alright.' I didn't know the half of it. The room spun and I was soon kneeling over the toilet bowl watching the procession of tomatoes, eggs, beans, whole beans mind you, that came all the way up from my stomach. 'Sunday tomorrow, I'll need it.'

Although at the time I swore I would never drink again, going to the pub became a regular event. I was walking home from the pub by myself one night and recognised Jamie up the road with a group of middle aged people, obviously his parents and family friends. They all disappeared into an underground station. I had to go through the station myself to get across the road. I could see them all as I descended the stairs. They were saying goodbye. Jamie and his parents disappeared from view down the escalators. It was a few seconds before the strangeness of it all penetrated my senses. They were shaking hands, kissing, smiling and waving but they were not talking. They were using their hands to make gestures. Except for Jamie they were all deaf and dumb, mute. I could not believe it. Jamie had never mentioned it to me in school. I thought he had not seen me but when I saw him again the next morning in the classroom I was not sure. His eyes seemed to be saying, 'Don't tell anybody.' I didn't and I never spoke to him about it either. All those years I had known him and never said a word, never even hinted. It had answered my mental question as to why his parents never came to open day or meetings.

The pub was not a weekly thing at first. I could not afford it. It was alright for the others with a tenner a week as apprentices. I still had to get by on pocket money. I managed to have one or two at the local and sometimes went mad and overdid it. Many days I had to face my schoolwork with a hangover.

All during term we were seeing careers officers. My one laughed when I told him I wanted to be a journalist and told me I would need 'A' levels, 'O' levels at least and I was only taking C.S.E.s that year. I decided to stay on for the sixth. I had promised myself I would not when I joined the school but I did not know what to do anyway and if I took 'O' levels maybe they might come in handy.

Mr. Price, with little notebook in hand, visited the two top classes to have an informal discussion about the boys' future plans.

He managed to get annoyed at some of the answers even though the boys who would have answered 'I want to be a professional footballer' had left at the end of the fourth.

'What do you want to be Pablo?'

'Screen star.'

Even Mr. Price tolerated this–everybody knew Pablo. The boy behind Pablo was not so lucky. When he answered 'Undertaker' to the same question Mr. Price felt he had been mocked enough and proceeded to batter the poor boy against the walls. The boy had been telling the truth of course. His father and his father before him had all been undertakers.

'It's a dying trade.'

'You're always the last to let someone down.'

'How can you bear to work with all those stiffs?'

He had to put up with it for years.

Nobody on the staff asked me at all what I wanted to do and I was a bit worried. I told one of the teachers I did not know what job I wanted. 'Then you must be even dumber than you look,' he told me.

The fifth year was the last in the tutor group. We would have our own room next term and I was elected head of S3. Besides some instantly forgettable duties and falsifying the credit register, the main job was to keep the kids quiet while the teacher was out of the room.

The lecture theatre, which doubled as S3 tutor room, had a series of steps with benches on each one facing the front. One particular boy, a black boy, kept drumming with his hands and tapping his feet.

'Quit the noise up there,' I said, a trifle aggressive.

He didn't and got louder. It was a hot day and thoughts about jobs, C.S.E's and pints filled my head. I erupted immediately.

'You stop that bloody banging,' I shouted, 'or I'll flatten you.'

'Fuck off,' said the boy.

It was my confrontation with Mr. Coombs again except I was playing the part of the teacher. I bounded up the steps and grabbed hold of the boy's blazer. He gyrated and leapt up. I raised a fist to his face. And then we stopped. We both looked at each other, very tense. Everybody else was watching us. 'Anything the matter?' said our tutor master. He had entered silently behind us. 'Nothing,' I answered still looking at the infuriated boy.

Perhaps that's what growing up means: becoming all the things you ever despised.

More of the long arm law

And so on to the sixth form where most of us who had not
committed serious crimes or acts of grave indiscretion, or had not
been caught, were made into prefects.

Our C.S.E. results were through. We compared grades.

'I never got any grade ones,' I said.

'Idiot,' said Paul. 'I got a grade one, the rest are twos and
threes.'

'I've got some bloody fours and fives 'ere,' I confided. 'I
wouldn't get a job at OZ with these.'

Jamie left that year. Jamie, the life and soul of the classroom.
It was shyness again that prevented us from shaking hands. In fact
we probably did not even say goodbye. It was a lazy year and a
happy one at first. We got away with murder. We were even
honoured with our own private lavatory, the executive status
symbol. We were all provided with a bright silver key which got
lost and made going for a pee hard work. Unfortunately with
white tiled walls would-be graffiti artists never got a chance.
They were washed down regularly and its patrons' messages to the
world and mankind were lost forever. A shame really, maybe it
was their only chance. Anyway, we also had our own sixth form
room with a record player, got to sit at the back of the stage
behind the teachers in assemblies and went home when we wanted.
We were not supposed to but most teachers were not over
bothered. We did not do games, P.E. or anything requiring even
the minimum of physical exertion.

Being a prefect, however, did mean more than getting a red
striped tie. We had to police the school in an Inspector
Clouseau manner and be a general hindrance to the enjoyment
of the lower years. All other years except the new fifth year that
is. Unlike any year before us, and for no apparent reason other
than that we all had long hair, we formed an alliance with them
and let them break the same rules we did.

The wind of change by that time had blown strong through the
school corridors and we were greeted more often than not with a
two-fingered salute and 'Fuck you' rather than any school cap
forlock tugging. In my first year the sixth formers had looked
so menacing to us, but now it was the first years we spent all our
time avoiding. I was put in charge of the back gate and had to stop
anyone escaping during the lunch hours. I may have stopped one
or two at the start but I soon got bored and let everyone go out
to the sweetshop, the chip shop or home.

The only prefect duty we really enjoyed was keeping the other years out of the building during break. It was like a scaled down Colditz except we had to use all our wits to keep the kids out, not in. They would climb in the building at the start of break, in which case we had to rout them out like stormtroopers. We would burst open doors to the rooms they squatted in and throw them outside into the rain, snow or hail. Never being a subtle crowd of boys, the most common form of attempted entry was through the main doors. A particular group of second years took it to mind to try and batter them down daily. The lock was a long time broken and often they would push it open just enough for a few small boys to dribble in beneath our straining arms. Once in a particularly nasty confrontation I started to kick out at the little invaders through the open double doors only to have my 'colleagues' shut them hard on my ankles. I never did that again.

It was time for us to use the Long Arm Law. Prefects were usually bigger than anyone else and we had might on our side. It has often been said that by putting a man in uniform you bring out all his worst aspects, power-craving and militarism. The same was true of that red striped tie. Keyhole Kate was certainly not what I would have called the violent type, but ..... We were patrolling the corridors one lunch hour when we saw a small group of boys coming up the stairs. We stood at the top, 'Go back down you lot,' said Kate. The boys kept coming. Kate kicked the first boy in the stomach and then punched him in the face with a right hook. I could not believe it. There was a scuffle to remove the boys by both of us but it was Kate who had done it all. The red tie had totally transformed him. He was a somebody now, someone who needed to be shown respect.

We had a new Headmaster that year. He was a tall tidy man with gaunt pale features. It was not long before Pablo got him off to a tee and likened him to Dracula as played by Christopher Lee.

The old Head had left the school with a standing ovation and a stereo unit bought out of a school collection. Mr. Epstein, his successor, was not very well liked from the start. He was stiff, silent and aloof and we soon found ourselves saying, 'The old Head wasn't so bad after all was he?'

Over the year we found we lost more than we started with. The coffee machine was returned because of the state we got it in and our loo honour was taken away. What happened was this. Keyhole Kate had lost his key and was dying for a pee. Rather than mix with the riff-raff in the other loos, he waited for someone else to open up the door. Unfortunately it was Patrick O'Hooligan who opened the door and for a laugh, which was all he was ever interested in, he locked Kate in there when he went

out. Kate was in there for hours banging on the door, shouting
and so angry that he grassed .... nobody knew he was there.

Our Sixth Form Society was always watched over by a
teacher, albeit a sympathetic one. Our meetings were formless
and useless. We hardly ever discussed relevant issues and spent
literally a whole month of meetings on the introduction of
cherry pies in the sixth form room. We had elections every
couple of months and had a different president everytime — it
was like a South American government. One Friday in a bout of
outrageous silliness we elected Pablo as president. He actually
looked like a South American president.

The new Headmaster took an instant dislike to Pablo. Pablo
never wore school uniform, was loud, and had the thickest stubble
I've ever seen on a sixteen year old. It grew by the second: if he
was clean shaven when you saw him in the morning he had a
beard by the time you went home. Mr. Epstein first asked Pablo
to get rid of his beard, then requested him and then ordered
him. In the end he gave Pablo the ultimatum 'shave or leave'.
Pablo spent all day avoiding the Headmaster but somehow
always managed to turn a corner and meet him face to bearded
face.

Mr. Epstein also clamped down on the practice of going home
in free periods. He set up teacher look-outs and personally
chased Robin Jones out the back gate. Us prefects were told to
act in a more prefect-like way and that if we did not wear
complete uniform our prefect ties would be taken from us. We
were given assignments. Kids were supposedly wandering around
the block of flats opposite the school scaring the inhabitants. We
were sent over in twos to rout them out. We met another two
prefects and over the next few days more and more pairs. In fact
prefects were the only boys we ever saw there. We came to the
conclusion we were the boys we had been sent over to find.

It was the uniform that proved to be the last straw, or thread
I should say. A letter to Mr. Epstein was written on inky paper
in unintelligible scrawl applauding his stand on uniforms. It was
an obvious piss-take and was signed by Pablo. Pablo was innocent.
He had no part in it. He was framed. Nevertheless he was sent for
and told off and when he was finally proved innocent everybody
in the sixth form was sent for and told off. Nobody owned up
and we were told, 'You have forfeited your right to special
treatment, from now on you will be treated with no more
consideration or leniency than anyone else.'

STOP PRESS
Europe goes L.S.D.

Somebody had written that on the blackboard. It brought a

smile to the lips of everybody who saw it, and some even
believed it. Even Mr. Price smiled but scrubbed it off the
board with one brush of his duster. The new money had been
in since January 1st 1970 but we still had not got the hang of
it. On the wall opposite, a chart explained the meaning of
decimalisation. 'Innit bloody typical' said someone, 'they
spend ten bleedin' years teaching us how to add up 7/6½d
and 8s/11d and now at the last they change it all to suit the
bloody Frogs.'

Mr. Price gave us some consideration and leniency. True
to his legend the sixth form found Mr. Price a different man.
We were now cured of childhood and found we could speak
to him in an adult sort of way. He was witty and civilised
and let us in on the dirty bits in Shakespeare. He had a
burning passion for D.H. Lawrence and the intellectual ideals
of the turn of the century. Rumours filtered through of how
Mr. Price himself in the late thirties was something of a drop
out who had no desire in life other than to play the piano.
It all culminated however, and this was solid fact, in him
joining the air-force in time for World War Two and becoming
a Battle of Britain pilot. He never talked about it, except to
tell us what a stuck up little bastard he was at the time.

We were too big to hit now and although he still saw it as
essential for the other years he settled for adult comradeship
with us. One boy had not done any homework for a month.
Mr. Price said nothing all through the lesson but came over
and sat by the boy while the rest of us were putting our books
away and leaving.

'You haven't done any homework for a while have you?'
he said. The boy looked pretty depressed and turned away
shrugging his shoulders.

'I just can't seem to manage it,' he said, 'I got problems.'
The boy was looking down.

'So have I, boy,' said Mr. Price, seemingly incensed, 'so
have I.'

It was Mr. Price's job to lead us up to those 'O' level
examinations. He told us frankly that we would be taught
nothing that was not involved in the syllabus and that exams
merely dictated a set course and did not test how much you
really knew. There were a lot of things Mr. Price would have
liked to discuss but instead he had to use all our lessons and
energies to pass the exams.

There were only two classes in English in the sixth. There
were among us some fifth who were bypassing the C.S.E.'s
and a few upper sixth (second year sixth) who had failed or
missed the exam last year. Julian was one of this latter group.

Julian had been a friend of Danny's since the first year. We used to meet quite often but were not really friends. Now most of our other friends had left we saw more of each other. We lived quite near to each other, and started to go down to a new pub to talk and drink our under-age drinks.

On the first lesson that term, the only one Julian turned up to, Mr. Price gave us a pep talk.

'Now listen to me lads, I may be a bit ancient and have short hair but I hope you'll credit me with just a little bit of wisdom. We have only one more year left in this 'O' level course, English literature and English language. To pass these exams and indeed all other exams in other subjects you will have to study hard. When I say study I don't just mean in the classroom but at home as well. You must sacrifice your evenings to your books.'

I doubt if many of the boys in the class were thinking of becoming trainee hippies but Mr. Price obviously thought it was a possibility. His speech continued thus:

'It's a well known thing today that young people feel like dropping out. I beseech you not to do so, and I'll tell you why. It's not for the reasons you think. I don't personally care if half the population of British youth goes off to India to sit on a hill for the rest of their lives, it makes perfect sense to me. Why they want to ruin it with drugs I don't know, but that's another matter. Old standards are going by the board today, pomp, hypocrisy and a bloody good job too. I have a feeling though that the loud intellectual left are not as representative of your generation as certain people would have us suppose. I think though, that no matter what amount of rebellion or dropping out you do you will sometime or another want to join or rejoin society, or even the so called 'alternative society'. A good knowledge of the written word, regardless of exams, is essential today, and I'm sure even in the 'alternative society' intelligence and responsibility would be a great virtue. It's for your sake, certainly not mine, that I hope you stay on this course, stay interested and take the examinations.'

His body untensed and he smiled. 'So forget that extra pint the next time you're out boozing and remember what this old man said.'

I turned my head slightly and gave a side-long glance to Julian at the mention of booze; he was already grinning at me.

We used to drink together while we were at school and it was a convention we upheld later on as well. I got on even better with Julian after we had left school actually and we spent a lot of our evenings in the pub talking about nothing else but the old days in school. It was as if the outside world had not caught up with us yet. I thought of Gulliver's Travels. We had worked our way up through Primary school to become the biggest boys and then done it again at Effingham Road and now we were small again in the world of work.

I went to an interview for a Commercial Art company off Fleet Street before my 'O' level results were through. They did not even ask about them. It was only eight pounds a week and I didn't go to day release college. This was the only way in they said, work your way up from the bottom. I did not even know what went on there. I just had the vague notion it might be more interesting and varied than being an accountant or something. The title of the job was Trainee/Messenger but I seemed to be doing a hell of a lot of messengering and none of the training.

It was 1971 and the summer of the OZ magazine trials. There was a demonstration going on just up the road and I felt I ought to be there. I was trapped at work though, physically and probably mentally as well. I had already stopped doing the Task Force jobs. Charity didn't seem to fit into this new world. The outside world was such a disappointment after all that school preparation for it.

It was about six months after leaving school after a typical weekday booze up. I had had a few pints and was tired. I could not wait to get home to bed. I had said goodbye to Julian at the corner and was halfway down the wide road which would eventually lead me home. Suddenly and with damn good braking a car pulled up about fifty yards ahead of me.

A dozen motives for its halt went through my mind. They were a gang of yobs who wanted to beat me up. They were motorized muggers or maybe it was a rich widow looking for a stud. As I walked by the back door they would spring open and a heavily jewelled finger would beckon me in.

I decided to play safe and cross over to the opposite side of the road. Before my foot hit the gutter however another car, the type with a bright revolving light on top, screeched to a halt behind me.

Three plainclothes policemen jumped out of the first car and one of the uniformed type from the one behind me. They did not ask for permission to search me or show any warrants but they were not really rough either. It just all happened so quickly. They did it all just perfectly, like the American TV detectives. They sorted through my pockets, felt up my legs and checked my wrists.

'What's this?' said one.

'It's a watch,' I told him.

In my jacket pocket they found a length of flex that I had bought that day for a record player. I prayed to God that nobody had been strangled that night.

Again, I cannot remember any pushing or shoving but I soon found myself, quite against my will, sitting in the first car's back seat. There were two policemen either side of me and two in the front, they were all staring at me, all except the driver that is, who turned the car round and moved off in the direction I had come from.

I was shaking like a drenched cat and when they started the questioning it got worse: knees, teeth and elbows rattling like a kettle with a loose lid. Name? Address? Why are you here? Where have you been?

I wondered if they had picked up Julian as well, had been watching us and waited until we parted before picking us up individually, checking if our stories tallied.

The questions were coming thick and fast, some seeming quite irrelevant. 'Do you drink?' 'How much do you earn?'

I told them yes to the first, I had been in the pub all night. It was a pity I had already told them I was only seventeen but they didn't seem to notice.

'Have you ever been in trouble before?' said the blonde one in the front seat.

'Been in trouble before,' I thought, 'who said I was in trouble now?' All I said was a meek 'No'.

'You know I could check up on that right now don't you?' he said, 'I just have to call the station over the radio and find out just like that.'

'Go ahead then,' I said, 'I don't care.'

For the first time now I was angry. They actually doubted my word and up until now I had felt I was inconveniencing them.

He seemed surprised. His eyes asked 'Are you bluffing?'

As yet I still did not know what I was supposed to have done. I would never be told.

'Who was you in the pub with?'

'A friend.'

'Name?'

There was no reason for fear, we had done nothing wrong. So why did I feel like a coppers nark when I gave them his name?

'His address?'

It must have sounded suspicious. I couldn't tell them his address. I knew Julian's flat and how to get there. I had been there many times but I honestly did not know the bloody address.

The car had pulled into a side street and stopped. There was much activity outside a large house on the other side of the road. All the lights were on and police were everywhere. A policeman came across from the house and leaned in through the window. He looked at me the way I look at dogshit.

'You know where we are don't you?' the blonde guy said to me.

'What?' I croaked.

'You cold or something?' the one beside me said.

'What?'

'I wondered why you're shaking so much.'

'I'm scared,' I told him.

'If you're innocent you've got nothing to worry about have you?' he said.

Now the policeman to my other side in a hoarse, calculated voice, 'Two fellas were seen leaving that house tonight and one of 'em fits your desciption. In fact he was wearing a coat exactly like yours.' He held my sleeve in his fingers.

'That's my hard luck,' I said.

The other one was suddenly reasonable:—

'Now listen son,' he said, 'we've got alsation dogs in that house over there sniffing about. An' if you've been in there tonight your scent is going to be everywhere, 'an those dogs are smart, they'll recognise you straight off, don't you worry about that.' He paused for dramatic effect. 'Now in a minute we're going to bring those dogs over to you an' if they recognise you they'll tear you apart, and we won't stop them.'

He waited for a frantic tearful confession but he didn't get one. There was a tap on the window and he got out. No dogs, but two policemen with torches grabbed my feet and swung my legs out of the car. They inspected the soles of my shoes and for several seconds, mumbled and looked at each other. The blonde policeman in the front was looking at my face all the time.

The dog lover got back in, exchanged a few words with the driver and the car burst into life.

As we drove off and swung round close to the house I saw a frail old lady on the doorstep. A police woman was beside her. The crackling radio provided the only conversation on the ride back to where they had found me. At the red lights the dog lover jumped out and said to me, 'O.K.' That meant 'Get out and go home. Just think of all the time we've wasted on you and you didn't even do it.' No apologies. No ride home and thankfully no alsations either.

He got back in and the door slammed. The cars went off in search of others.

I was dying for a pee and walked home quickly. I had visions of them following me home and searching the house. A million tales of police harassment flooded my mind. Big Brother's eyes were burning a hole in my neck.

The next morning my mother went over to the Police Station to complain about this treatment of her son. The desk sergeant talked her round though.

'He was a nice chap,' she said.

I was sitting in an armchair all day expecting a raid. It never happened. They had not picked Julian up either, he had gone off down a side turning and had missed them by seconds.

Oh, in case you are wondering, no, I did not do whatever had been done. Honest.

The Contemptible Arts Society

Young men, lithe and long haired, plugged into the wall–a vision of heaven or hell? I'm not sure which.

Julian introduced us to the Sunday concerts at 'The Big Tower', a converted depot of some sort which was now a theatre during the week but a rock venue on a Sunday. It was just a bus ride away.

'You ve got to come to the Tower this week,' he told me in school on Friday, 'it's great. They've got the best rock groups in the whole of London and it's only fifty pence to get in. Not only that, it's from three in the afternoon 'till midnight.' Being a bit wary I did not go at first but when Danny told me he was going along too I decided I could not be left out.

If I was wary before I went to the Tower, I was even more wary when I saw the queue outside. It stretched all the way around the block and consisted entirely of young men and women with long hair, lank, loose, tied up at the back or frizzed out. They were clothed in a selection of Afgans, Kaftans, T shirts and faded patched jeans.

All four of us waited for an hour and slowly the long line moved further up the high wooden steps. 'We were lucky we got here early', said Julian. 'I had to wait for two hours last week.'

Inside, the music was deafening. I entered and paid my money and a man put a rubber ink stamp on my hand. 'What's that for?' I asked Julian. 'That's instead of a ticket. It's so that you can go out and come back in again without any hassle,' he explained.

The central area of the Tower had a low stage at one end and no chairs. Just the stone floor and a few graduated steps to sit on. We walked around the foyer looking at the people and catching snatches of conversation. It was crowded with stalls run by pretty girls and men with beards. They sold beads, mock jewellery, badges, scents , crucifixes and occult hexs. Another may have books on the lost eastern mystical cults, it was that sort of place.

Soft drugs were a currency and men of smoke sat crouched in all the nooks and crannies of the place, and there were many. I did not know what any of it all meant and if I was ever asked if I wanted to score I thought they were talking about football.

There was a counter which sold huge bread rolls

crammed with food at very cheap prices. No beer though.
The stamp on the hand was a good idea after all. When an
unbearable group came on we went out to the pub, downed
a few pints with the burly Irish regulars and hurried back.

The place throbbed. A group was letting fly with drum
solos, guitar breaks and frothing at the mouth. The group
would be bathed in the best psychedelic light show in
Britain. Liquid blobs, brightly coloured, would crawl over
the walls along with images of Eden and Jimi Hendrix. All
together, pounding and thudding, lightening and brightening,
it would stab at the ears, eyes and backside, the floor getting
harder. The loudest sound known to man outside Concorde
knocked at our ear drums and made talk below a shout
impossible.

People were up and dancing too, hips and hair flying out
in a disjointed mad flight. Smells of joss sticks or unknown
foreign scents accosted the nostrils and forced entry up into
the brain, squatting there and having a party. There was a
room where they showed films on a small projector. It was
something to go and see when the groups got boring and when
the films got boring we went back to see the groups.

The Tower was a place to get lost in but still some people
stood out from the rest. The lank-haired youth whose name
was 'jesus' who danced all night long, the black man with an
afro full of burning joss sticks. It had the effect in the dark
of making him look like a flourescent porcupine. He had a
much needed friend who removed the burnt down sticks
from his smouldering hair. And there were two painted girls
who never let go of each other's hands.

Late at night when the place had emptied out a bit, men
and girls who had had too much of whatever sat on the
stairs with their heads in hands or curled up in the corners
with friends around them, or just wandered around the
audience in a haze of purple lights treading on people's
hands and feet.

Towards the end of the evening Danny, Joe and Julian
went to the lavatory and left me sitting alone. A man in a
holed jumper came and sat down beside me, rubbed his
head a few times and turned to face me. 'Would you have
any cigarettes?' he asked me politely. 'No,' I told him,
'I'm sorry.' 'O.K. man,' he said and got up to try his luck
with someone else. I heard him behind me staggering
backwards and forwards almost losing his balance. Thinking
he had walked a long way and was over the other side of
the theatre somewhere, he sat down on the other side of
me, rubbed his head and asked, 'Would you have any

cigarettes, man?'

A few times in later weeks we would meet Robin Jones here and he would always have a long legged girl with him. None of us mentioned school here.

By the time everything had finished there was nothing we wanted to do except go home. So dodging the drunks and running for the last bus we returned home to our parents and bed, not bothering to tell them about the night we had. Lying on the bed with my smokey head on the crisp white pillow I would reflect on it all. The electric hum of guitars still rung in my ears.

It was about that time that Robin began to tell people that he was Marc Bolan's brother and it was because of his brother's overshadowing fame that he could not get in on the music business. With me as a sometimes unwilling sidekick he visited the Soho folk cellars and would present himself on stage at the slightest hint of an invitation. He showed me how playing a guitar gets you free drinks and a head start in picking up the girls.

Robin Jones craved fame, just a little, just enough to live on and sustain him like bread and water. It was either in this overwhelming desire or a genuine belief in Effingham Road Comprehensive culture that he suggested the formation of a school Arts group. The Contemporary Arts Society was the name he had mooted for it. It was in his interests because as singer-songwriter-guitarist he claimed he should start off each meeting with about half an hour of his songs. A few of the teachers thought it was a good idea too. It would help break down teacher-pupil barriers they said.

In that year there was also much talk of launching a school magazine. A four page pamphlet was circulated once a month by one of the houses but it only seemed to concern itself with past and forthcoming sports events. Our magazine would be different. Articles about everything by everyone would appear without fear of reprisals or reprimand. 'No censorship' we all said, both pupils and younger staff. I thought I would like to contribute to it by writing an article. I don't know what attracted me to writing in the first place. I think maybe because I wanted to let people know, ever so gently, that I wasn't an idiot.

I was invited, or self-elected, to write an article for the first issue. In fact I wrote two and of course I wrote about the Contemporary Arts Society.

'In a school of many people like Effingham Road there are bound to be many different tastes among the pupils which have to be catered for. In this school it has been done satisfactorily so far as sport and discussion groups but never before has it had a successful arts group of the type like the Contemporary Arts Society.

With Robin Jones and Mr. Davies in the forefront of the organization, the society came to life in late 1970 and it was decided then that it would be mainly concerned with folk music. Even before the first meeting however the idea developed and it was agreed among members that a much wider spectrum of the arts should be involved. So, when attending a meeting one could expect to find live folk music, recorded music, poetry and a lecture on any aspect of any art form.

So far the society has only been open to sixth formers. It is felt it is best kept small so one can feel at home among friends and not afraid to 'Do his own thing.' Anybody is allowed to perform or say what he likes because there is no board which decides what can and cannot be done, instead everybody there becomes the society and is encouraged to do something. Very recently girls from St. Cilla's Convent have been invited to our meetings and it is hoped will broaden our activities. Every meeting is begun by Robin Jones who breaks the ice by singing a few of his own compositions or those of Bob Dylan or Leonard Cohen. Poetry is provided by regular attender Mr. Akinfield and Frank Long who reads his own work. The poems vary greatly in subject, they could be funny, sad, beautiful or horrific, either way they are enjoyable. What records are played is determined by what is brought by the sixth. So far records by the Band, The Velvet Underground, Pink Floyd, Credence Clearwater Revival and The Who have all been played and given satisfaction to some if not all members.

Members of staff also contribute by giving a talk on a subject in which they are interested. Mr. Cooper may best be known as an Art master but he is also a knowledgeable blues fan. In March he gave us a talk illustrated with records of the period on this American music form and explained how it is still enjoyed by the underprivileged coloured workers who make the songs up to play and sing to friends. Recordings played dated back to the 1920s and '30s (dispelling the rumour that the blues began with Eric Clapton)..

Mr. Price also obliged a request and gave a very interesting lecture making a comparison between classical and modern music. He did this by playing the piano and records and explained the methods used by a composer when setting poetry to music. Among his examples he played pieces by Benjamin Britten and Bob Dylan.

For lectures in the future we hope to have Mr. Davies on James Joyce and Mr. Gogh on the nude in Art.

It is hoped that next year the new sixth will continue the Contemporary Arts Society. It is hoped that like this year the boundaries will continue to widen and that more and more interests will be taken into account.'

All lies. The facts were true of course but rather than grow and grow as I made it sound, the attendance dwindled after the first few months. By the time Mr. Price gave his lecture there was just about three of us in there to see it. Even after going public and allowing fifth formers in we were a bit lonely.

That was when we invited the St. Cilla's schoolgirls. If they couldn't boost membership nothing could. That plan backfired because they all turned up with guitars and in the end anyone who wasn't a 16th century Northumberland folk song enthusiast didn't feel welcome. Robin started to do epic stints of his own compositions and the society started to be called the *Contemptible* Arts Society. It ended in Robin being kidnapped and locked in a cupboard after one particularly excruciating session.

Via *Time Out* in the school library I learned of *The Little Red Schoolbook*. We never did get to discuss it in the society but I thought it would make an excellent subject for the proposed school magazine which as the months progressed was being less and less discussed.

> ' I make no apologies in this article for reviewing a book I have not read. The seizing of this book by the authorities has made it impossible for me to do so. It is for the same reason therefore that I make no judgement but merely pass on its advice and information in a series of extracts which I have culled from other publications.
>
> The book is relevant to schoolchildren everywhere, and that's you.
>
> The Little Red Schoolbook was first published in Denmark. "The frank and detailed information it presented to children made it an educational bombshell" claim the publishers. However it is not anarchistic nor, as Conservative MP Gerald Nabarro and Mary Whitehouse seem to think, will it deprave and corrupt the children of the nation.
>
> Although the press highlighted the fact that it offers advice on sex and drugs they did not mentioned that the book is anti-drugs and that its advice on sex is mere common sense.'

I then went on to quote passages from the book. The teacher I showed it to looked quite shocked.

'Well you know, this doesn't really apply to the school,' he said. 'It applies to all schools,' I answered a bit smugly.

He was after all a very new teacher and I knew that it was the Headmaster's reaction to the article that he was afraid of. Anyway the article I had written about the infamous Contemporary Arts Society was selected and it was decided that should be the one to go into print. It never did however. The magazine idea fell to pieces and everybody interested in it left at the end of that year. Me too.

The school I hear now does have a magazine in fact, a conventionally controlled one, but no Contemporary Arts Society. Not in its old form anyway. I myself took over its organization in its dying weeks at the end of term and by the next year it was forgotten.

Marking time

In that last year at Effingham Road there was certainly a feeling of marking time. It was the run up to those 'O' level examinations. I never revised. I figured that if I did not know it now I never would. At lunch times and throughout the day we took to going over to Tony's Cafe on the corner opposite the school.

Tony and his mother, always unseen and cooking furiously upstairs, ran the cafe in a friendly Italian manner. In their unique way they would serve up the kind of food it had taken generations to perfect. Egg, chips, beans, sausages and fried bread. It was cheap anyway. It was Tony's Cafe we went to for elevenses when school got drab ; and a cup of tea provided better refreshment than the water from the bog taps.

One day it was different. We opened the door, we went in, saw the chairs, saw the tables and the out of date nudie calendar on the dirty wall. Something was missing though. Tony was bloody missing that's what. Tony, his mother and everybody else. Tony's Cafe was up for demolition because of the new roundabout and they had gone overnight. Never more would we sit, eat, drink, argue and eye up the birds from our table by the window.

I wish now that I had tipped him at least once.

There was nowhere else to go. There was the chip shop, the Wimpy Bar or the place up the road where they always gave you someone else's meal, but we had tried them all. No, only Tony had been able to provide the charming tatty service we required.

We took to buying beigels from the Jewish bakers and eating them back at school, or sometimes we took a ride in Patrick O'Hooligan's car which would unexpectedly come sleeking from a side street. A shout or a whistle from Patrick with his hands confidently round the wheel and his brother with him and we would jump in the back seat.

'Does you Dad know you've got his car Pat?'
'Oh he won't even be up as yet.'
'How long have you been driving?'
'It would be just a few months now I should think.'
'A few months! It takes that long for the test to come up.'
'That's right. I must put in for one of those things.'

'You've no license?!'

'No, but don't you be worrying, me father's got one and it's his car,' he smiled.

'Oh that's good.'

When we were not looking for a cafe, at Clissold Park or gone home, it was not unheard of for us to actually use the school library in our free periods. The librarian was a pretty petite blonde and they stocked the new fortnightly 'Time Out' and that was enough. The library was divided into two parts, an annexe which we contrived to keep for our exclusive use, even resorting to barricades, and the main library where classes were held.

I was reading more all the time. I read Orwell's 1984 and enjoyed it but got over-ambitious and one week took out 'The Castle' by Franz Kafka. I took it back again the next morning.

It was Mr. Scot's class there that made us older pupils think hard and long. The library was not a classroom, the desks were not in rows and Mr. Scot was surrounded by boys rather than at the head of them. In Mr. Scot's library class boys smoked, played cards, told him to bugger off and once even punched him. The reedy Scotsman ran around the room, screamed at the top of his voice and ran his fingers through his hair. It was a shame. We knew Mr. Scot was a reasonable man to speak to but he was not given the chance to teach purely because the kids were shouting so loud they could not hear him.

Watching it all from our annexe, I thought back to my days here and remembered how quiet, how servile we had been, and that scraping our chairs in the musty silence had been an offence worthy of being put out of the room. Something very dramatic had occurred in those years between 1965 and 1971.

That year the 'Professor' took us on quite a few outings, to museums to get lost in and on boat trips up the river that he slept through. The final trip was to Runnymede. He showed us the site where the Magna Carta was signed and explained how it had once been isolated by marshland and showed us the column some American lawyers had stuck there.

I enjoyed the ride in the coach the best. It was an opportunity for us London boys to see those rolling hills and fat cows the poets were always writing about. Even the air smelt different out there. We stopped at an ancient mill along the way, still operated by the flowing river nearby. The people working there seemed just as ancient. There were three of them, all tubby, cheerful men with just a foot in the twentieth century. These people looked different, spoke different and maybe even thought different. As a roadsign sharply reminded me however, we were still only a few miles out of London.

The last stop before returning was a World War Two Memorial: a large roofless construction with walls, columns and plinths covered in the names of the dead. A young man brushed past us hurriedly as we went in. As we went further in we saw some fresh flowers that he must have left there. What had he been in such a hurry about. Was he embarrassed? Maybe it was a father he had never known that he was commemorating, a father who had died at a younger age than he was himself. It must be strange, I mused, to think of your father as an immature young tearaway.

We were assembled, counted and put back on the coach. The 'Professor' told the driver to hold on a second.

'I'll make a promise not to go on too long,' he said. 'You owe a debt,' he told us, 'for the war. But you don't owe it to us,' he put his hand on his chest. 'You owe it to the next generation, your own children,' his voice raised for the first time and his spotlight eyes darted about for a challenge. 'You owe it to them to make sure your father's sacrifice was not a wasted one.'

He continued in this vein for a little while adding that even as he spoke now, people of all political shades were once again finding what they thought justification for murders.

There was utter silence as the Professor turned and nodded to the driver. The engines cracked the mausoleum silence like a twenty-one gun salute. If we thought we saw a tear in the Professor's eye then we didn't say so.

After the mock exams and Christmas they dedicated the last period on Wednesday in our annexe to careers lectures. They brought along a guest each week to give us a specialised talk. We had talks on a variety of jobs: Accountancy, Catering, Building, Shopkeeping. We had people from London Transport, from the GPO, and the LEB. We got taken on a few special careers outings, not at all like the professor's voyages of discovery.

The first trip was to a large car manufacturer's, a huge black shed where men stood on assembly lines and screwed on nuts and other men tightened them. We could hear nothing but an infernal din. It was my view of what hell must be like, thousands of men doing heartless, soul-destroying jobs without so much as a window to look out of. If we had not been in the middle of nowhere I think I would have walked out of that place, walked out into the fresh air and among the trees where you could feel carefree and human again, not an obliged pair of hands.

When the guide took us to a quiet room to talk to us I didn't even listen.

Another week we were taken to the teaching centre of a large London Bank group. We were shown how science had rescued banking from the eighteenth century but told that working in a bank was not as easy as it looked. Sometimes, they told us they were working away till eight o'clock at night. That was supposed to encourage us to join?

At the end of the tour we were placed in a lecture room and told , as if it were some sort of honour , that the director of the whole place was going to talk to us. He entered the room with all the pomp of a Lord Mayor, then just to show how he was not as straightlaced as he was he sat precariously on the edge of a table, his huge bulk straining the table legs and his waistcoat buttons. The man must have been about the same age as my father, but unlike my father he was fat and smooth skinned. His teeth were white and perfect, and his thinning hair neatly cut. He put his podgy hands on top of each other on his leg. The hands were like inflated rubber gloves, smooth, never cut and blistered by hard manual work.

The fat man told us all about the role of the modern bank, its whys and wherefores, why they were needed and why they were so important. It was stuff straight out of leaflets and again I was not listening. I couldn't stop looking at his hands. He condescended to answer questions at the end of his little speech and explained the actual work of the junior banker and his routes of promotion, how graduated pension works and how we could all become managers. When asked about the sort of person they wanted , and appearance, he explained how banks were so much more liberal nowadays but you couldn't expect a job if you turned up with hair down to your shoulders now could you?

Neither the physical nor the white collar jobs I had so far seen had really impressed me. Factories and the production line were right out and I did not like the work or stigma attached to an office either, 'pen-pushing' we called it. Both types of jobs involved working on a cycle of which you did not see the beginning or the end. But who did I think I was? I was sixteen, living in Hackney, a handful of C.S.E.s and no guarantee of getting 'O' levels in the forthcoming exams.

I did not really mind the exams, the mocks or the real thing. I was going in for five 'O' levels: English Literature, English Language, Commerce, Social Studies and Art. Although I had done so badly in my Maths C.S.E. the teacher said I may as well try the 'O' level course and he held special evening classes for us. I soon dropped out though and returned to the C.S.E. course. Just looking at the list of subjects now makes me wonder how I even got an eventual grade 4. There were: sets and venn diagrams, mode — mean and median, modulos, bases and binary, angles and bearings, trigonometry, areas and volumes, percentages, symmetry, fractions, algebra, properties of a circle, logarithmns, co-ordinances, formulas, linear programming, inequalities and mapping.

We had our examinations on little separate tables in the hall too far away from each other to copy. Strict silence was maintained throughout the two and a half hours when your sum total knowledge on any one subject was put to the test. Mr. Flicker and Mr. Price were usually on patrol, they had no time for cheats.

With the sun streaming in through the windows I quite forgot all about the importance of the occasion. Some boys kept on going to the front for those additional pieces of paper while others struggled to fill a side. Some boys read through their question papers and then walked out and some had to be virtually dragged away from their pens when time was called.

But me? I can honestly say I didn't give a damn. This was the final hurdle set for me to jump over. If I fell at this one it made a waste of time starting at all, but I didn't care. Such was my attitude that I did not even try to cheat until the Maths. I wrote scraps of information on my hand which the moisture pulled off and I wrote on my sheet of green blotting paper which was unreadable after the ink had spread. I wrote an absolutely phenomenal amount in the back of my log book but before we went in the books were taken away and we were issued with clean ones.

Afterwards some of the boys would spend hours discussing the papers with each other, and from memory would dissect the whole thing and compare answers. But I just walked on, out the gate and home. Another exam in the afternoon. I could wait for the results.

We would not get our results through until about half way through the summer holidays and I would want a job before then. So what did it all matter? Danny told me they did not give a toss about qualifications where he worked, that you did not get a job because of bits of paper but if your face fitted and you didn't cause trouble.

In those last days I was spending whole days in my front room by myself just staring at the wall, evenings in the pub with Danny and Joe talking to them but with my mind elsewhere, and restless nights in bed with the same thing going through my mind, 'What do I want to do, what do I want to do?' I was filled with a seething anger but I couldn't figure out what I was angry about.

It was about here I was going to give this little autobiography a neat, conclusive yet phoney end. Life doesn't seem to be that well written however. Realisation of the school's effect on me would dawn in my mind and I would get a good night's sleep. I did not get any such illumination of course and still haven't. Even so I did feel at the time as if I had been promised something by the school. Exactly what the promise was is the only thing holding up the end of my tale.

I went out last night for inspiration, to the pub and friends of my age who went to similar or nearby schools. I asked them, 'Do you feel you were promised something in school you didn't get when you left?' One said, 'A job.' Another talked about them making our expectations too high. Another said we were promised nothing definite except maybe an ability to apply their ragbag of knowledge to the outside world. The last said that we had been given a fair education in an unfair society and that comprehensives ought to be as revolutionary as the public schools are elitist.

I just nodded at all the suggestions and comments, said I still didn't know what the promise was and that I would have another pint.

Epilogue 1975

I just walked to the old school. Even though it had been a wet day I felt I had to go. I went the long way through the park. It seemed a lot smaller than I remembered it. Maybe it is.

To get to the school I had to go under Effingham Road, through the ill-lit tunnels of the new roundabout. 'The biggest in London' the council proudly proclaimed. 'A mugger's paradise' the local papers replied.

I did not go in after all. I just walked past the gates slowly, looking to see anyone I knew. I didn't see anyone.

The gates, the walls, the buildings, all looked smaller. Everything looked smaller.

It was lunchtime and there were many schoolkids out in the street. Lots of immigrants. Fat boys, thin boys, bullies and weeds, same kids as I knew only different names.

The school passed quickly. I saw the gym with those ropes to the roof I never had the courage to climb all the way up and the swimming pool we all helped to build. I saw the chewing gum engraved in the playground floor and the bikesheds where I hear now they drink whiskey from the bottle instead of smoking.

I was on the way home again before I knew it. I went the same way I used to, quite on purpose.

I was shocked. All the houses were gone. Ugly, grey unfinished flats stood high on muddy ground. They had been pulling down houses to build building sites.

I got the urge to go there after I met Pablo in the rainy Stoke Newington streets a few days earlier. We found we were both out of work. He told me an amazing thing. Mr. Epstein, the Headmaster, had been harassing him right up to the finish about his beard and clothes. He told him that no matter what happened how he would not be allowed back the next year.

'I didn't tell my parents though,' said Pablo, 'what could I do for a job? So what I'd do is go out in the mornings in my school uniform and when they went out to work I'd sneak back in. Sometimes I was surprised by them coming home early. What I would do is hide under the bed or in the cupboard until I could sneak out. I'd be in the cupboard for hours sometimes. I kept it up for months. It all came out in the end when my mum complained to the school about not being invited to teacher-parent meetings. Of course they were told, 'Your son is not even a pupil here anymore.'

I still see Danny and Julian, but they are the only only ones. Joe moved away and stopped going out. Keyhole Kate and the rest of the supporting cast have, I presume, settled down in honest jobs, all except Nick. Robin got married and went to live in Australia. I saw Paul a few times after leaving but not for a long time now and oh yes, Christaki made a lone return from Cyprus. He wonders why now.

I have not seen Jamie since the day he left school.